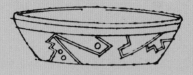

CRAFTS AND SKILLS
OF THE
NATIVE AMERICANS

CRAFTS AND SKILLS OF THE NATIVE AMERICANS

TIPIS, CANOES, JEWELRY, MOCCASINS, AND MORE

DAVID R. MONTGOMERY

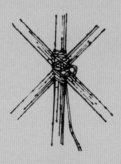

SKYHORSE PUBLISHING

Skyhorse Publishing books may be purchased in bulk at special discounts for sales promotion, corporate gifts, fund-raising, or educational purposes. Special editions can also be created to specifications. For details, contact the Special Sales Department, Skyhorse Publishing, 307 West 36th Street, 11th Floor, New York, NY 10018 or info@skyhorsepublishing.com.

Skyhorse® and Skyhorse Publishing® are registered trademarks of Skyhorse Publishing, Inc.®, a Delaware corporation.

Visit our website at www.skyhorsepublishing.com.

10 9 8 7 6 5

Library of Congress Cataloging-in-Publication Data

Montgomery, David R.
    Crafts and skills of the Native Americans : tipis, canoes, jewelry, moccasins, and more / by David R. Montgomery.
        p. cm.
    Includes bibliographical references and index.
    ISBN 978-1-60239-676-0 (alk. paper)
    1. Indian craft. 2. Indian arts—North America. 3. Indians of North America—Industries. I. Title.
    TT22.M644 2009
    745.5—dc22

                                    2009003774

Printed in China

CONTENTS

3. Weapons 39

4. Hunting, Tracking and Trapping 55

Animal Tracks

7. Cooking and Eating Utensils

8. Foods

9. Transportation

12. Bead and Quill Work 175

13. Musical Instruments and Games . 197

XI

CONTENTS

The Native Americans were a resourceful and ingenious people in the types of dwellings they chose to build and live in.

The Plains Indians developed a structure that was portable, warm in the winter, and cool in the summer. It could withstand the winds of the plains and could be packed on a travois with a moment's notice. The buffalo was the major raw material for the cover and dew cloth although elk and other hides were used. Lodge pole pine was generally used for the framework.

Anywhere from 10 to 20 hides were sewn together with sinew by tribe members who had the specific skills for tipi construction. Each tribe had their specific style but the tipis were all very similar. Crow Indians used a four-pole lodge as compared to the Cheyenne's three-pole lodge. The four-pole had shorter smoke flaps and a different cut in the base of the tipi. When white men introduced canvas, the tribes were quick to realize that this material was lighter in weight and much easier than buffalo hides to sew together.

Today, there is still no substitute for this first portable home. You can throw your 17 poles on top of your 250 or so horses (under the hood), pack the cover, dew cloth, pins, etc., inside and take off for high adventure with a very durable lightweight home.

The eastern Native Americans used earthen lodges and wigwams. The earthen lodges were constructed to maintain an even temperature and to house more than one family and sometimes even horses. They were dark inside with only the fire providing light. In the West, the early tribes of the Mogollon, Fremont, and Maidu lived in pit houses supported by a center pole with poles around the sides which were covered with thatch, mud,

CHAPTER 1
SHELTERS

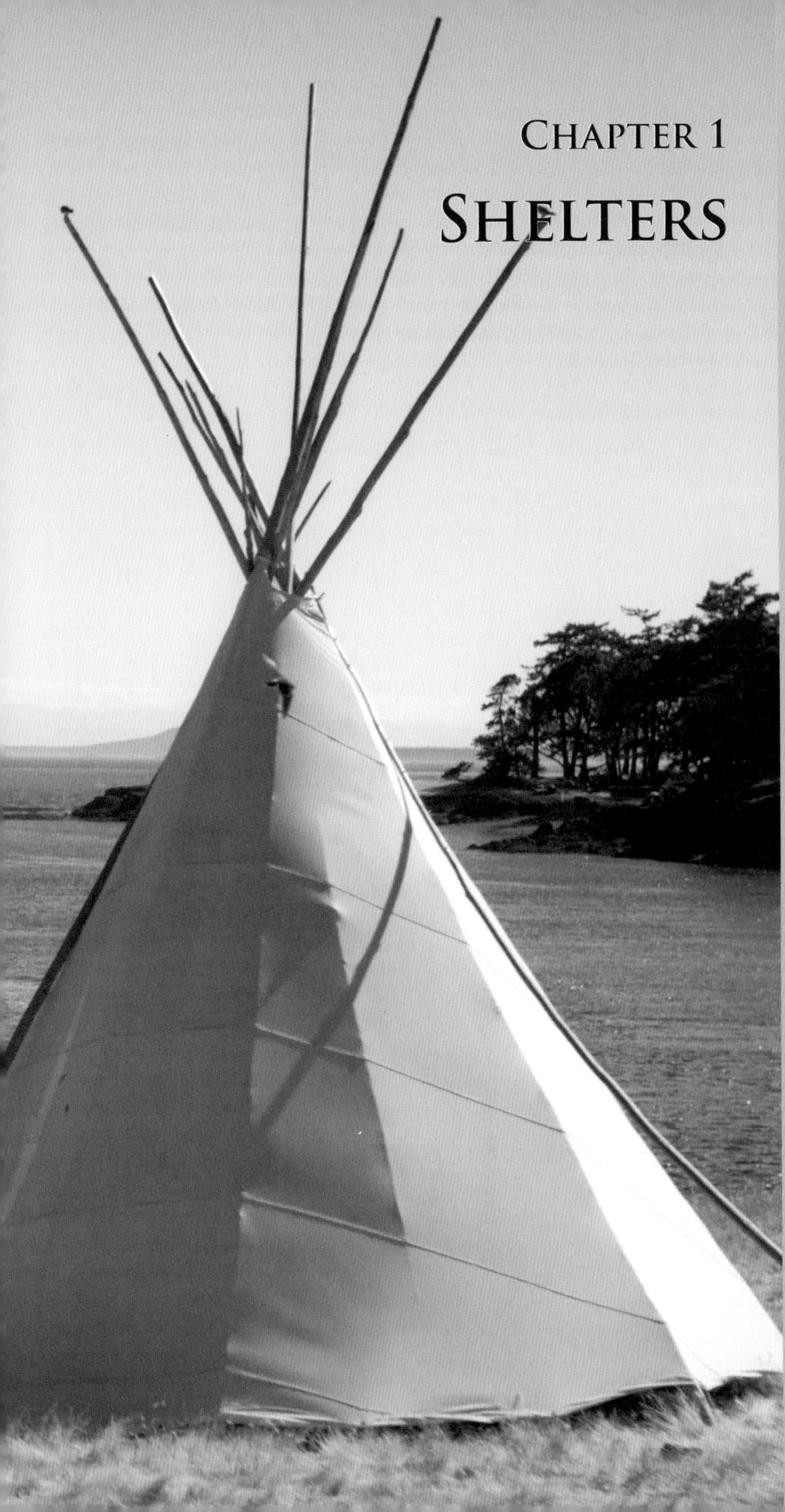

and sod. The wigwam was actually used in the North and upper West Coast as well as in the East and was built in a variety of shapes. Some were built with saplings then covered with birch bark. This was the best shape for a wigwam. Those that allowed for most use of space and retaining heat were the round and oval-shaped wigwams.

The western pueblos were constructed of stone, adobe, and wooden beams. Sometimes three and four levels were built on top of each other. These were nestled in large caverns in the cliff sides such as Arizona's Canyon de Chelly or Colorado's Mesa Verde. They also were constructed on the flat ground, as can be seen at Pueblo Bonito in New Mexico, or on a high mesa as was old Oribi in Arizona. Taos, New Mexico, and the pueblos of the Hopi such as Walpi, still house families whose ancestors lived there hundreds of years before.

Famine, wars, and disease caused many tribes to perish or to be dislodged from their natural homes and forced to live in a world that was—and is—in too much of a hurry to modernize. The shelters discussed in this section are only a few of the types that existed, but may be the ones which best suit your needs.

Various Native American Tribes

Tipi Construction

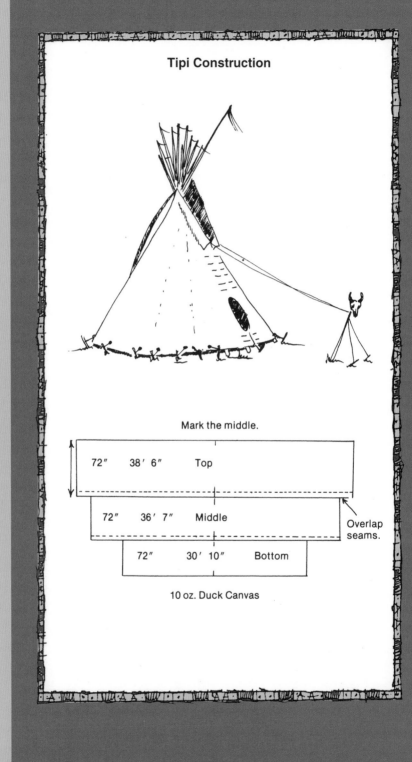

Mark the middle.

72″	38′ 6″	Top
72″	36′ 7″	Middle
72″	30′ 10″	Bottom

Overlap seams.

10 oz. Duck Canvas

Tipi Construction
(continued)
Top Strip

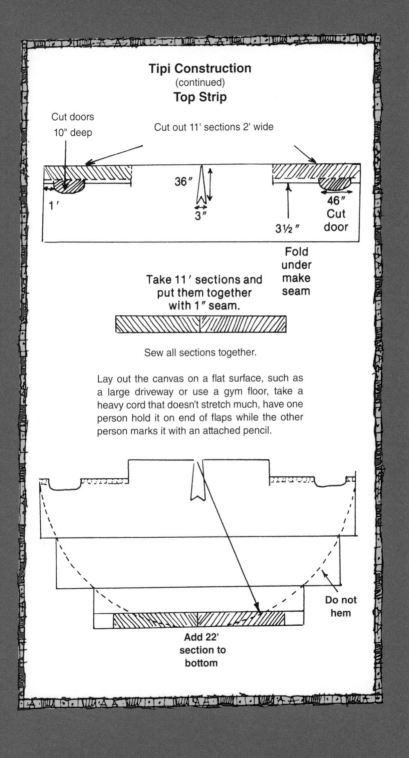

Cut doors 10" deep

Cut out 11' sections 2' wide

36"

3"

1'

46" Cut door

3½"

Fold under make seam

Take 11' sections and put them together with 1" seam.

Sew all sections together.

Lay out the canvas on a flat surface, such as a large driveway or use a gym floor, take a heavy cord that doesn't stretch much, have one person hold it on end of flaps while the other person marks it with an attached pencil.

Do not hem

Add 22' section to bottom

Tipi Construction
(continued)

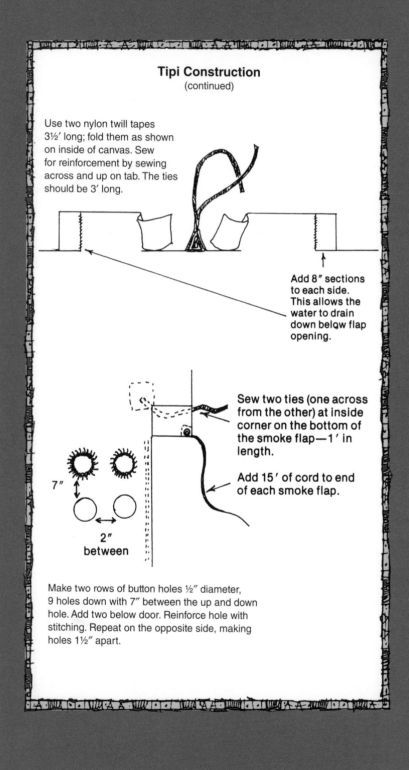

Use two nylon twill tapes 3½' long; fold them as shown on inside of canvas. Sew for reinforcement by sewing across and up on tab. The ties should be 3' long.

Add 8" sections to each side. This allows the water to drain down below flap opening.

Sew two ties (one across from the other) at inside corner on the bottom of the smoke flap—1' in length.

Add 15' of cord to end of each smoke flap.

7"

2"
between

Make two rows of button holes ½" diameter, 9 holes down with 7" between the up and down hole. Add two below door. Reinforce hole with stitching. Repeat on the opposite side, making holes 1½" apart.

Smoke Flap Pole Pocket

Use an 8″ section by 5½″ of canvas. Taper to top at 3″, fold over and double stitch. Sew cup so the pocket is on the outside of the top flap. Reinforce sewing to the flap. These pockets must take a lot of pressure. One on the upper outside of each smoke flap.

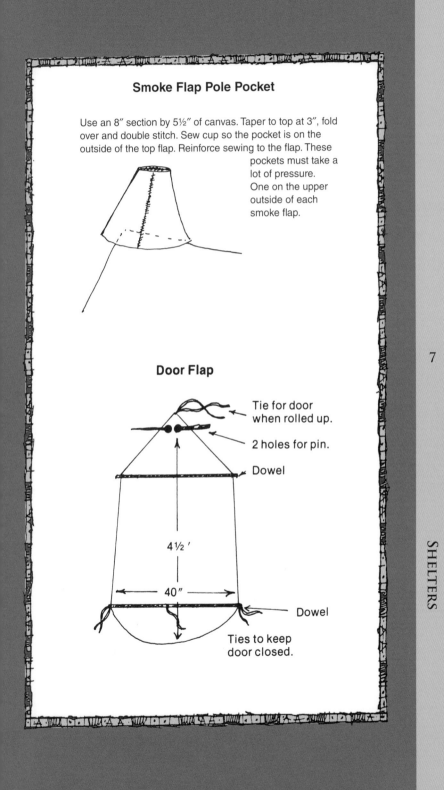

Door Flap

Tie for door when rolled up.

2 holes for pin.

Dowel

4½ ′

40″

Dowel

Ties to keep door closed.

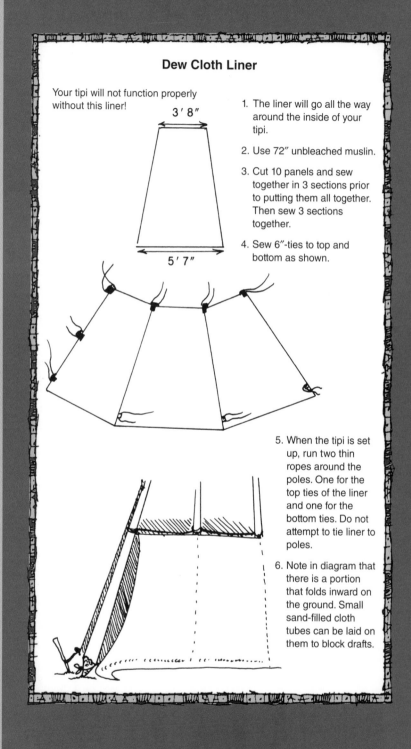

Dew Cloth Liner

Your tipi will not function properly without this liner!

3' 8"

5' 7"

1. The liner will go all the way around the inside of your tipi.

2. Use 72" unbleached muslin.

3. Cut 10 panels and sew together in 3 sections prior to putting them all together. Then sew 3 sections together.

4. Sew 6"-ties to top and bottom as shown.

5. When the tipi is set up, run two thin ropes around the poles. One for the top ties of the liner and one for the bottom ties. Do not attempt to tie liner to poles.

6. Note in diagram that there is a portion that folds inward on the ground. Small sand-filled cloth tubes can be laid on them to block drafts.

Setting Up the Tipi

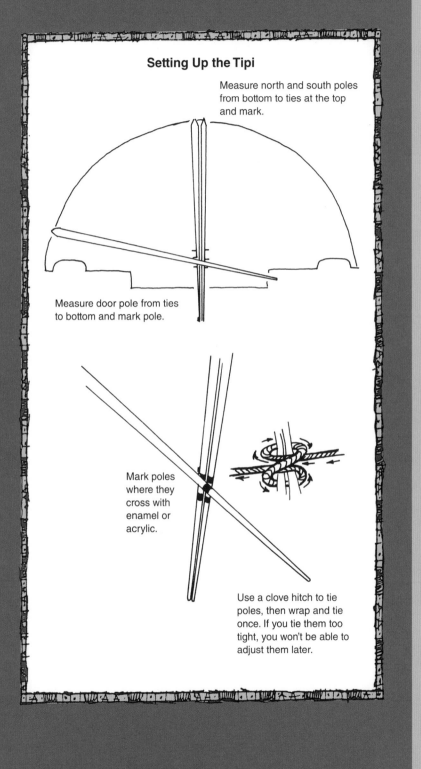

Measure north and south poles from bottom to ties at the top and mark.

Measure door pole from ties to bottom and mark pole.

Mark poles where they cross with enamel or acrylic.

Use a clove hitch to tie poles, then wrap and tie once. If you tie them too tight, you won't be able to adjust them later.

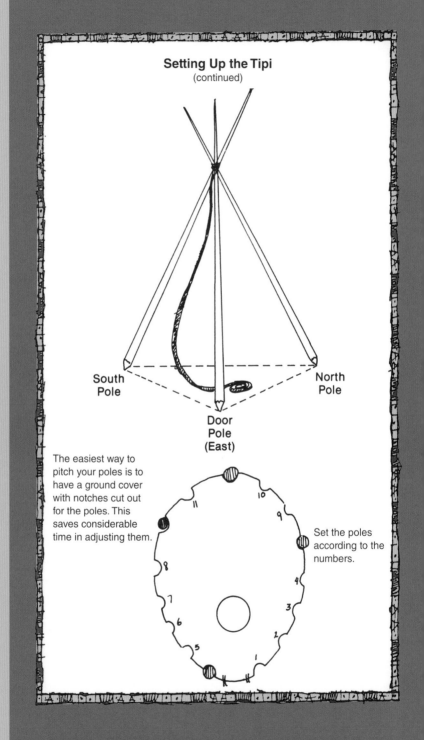

Setting Up the Tipi
(continued)

South Pole

North Pole

Door Pole (East)

The easiest way to pitch your poles is to have a ground cover with notches cut out for the poles. This saves considerable time in adjusting them.

Set the poles according to the numbers.

Setting Up the Tipi
(continued)

Once the poles are tied
down, tie the top of the
tipi to the mark on the lift
pole. If someone is helping,
have them put their foot on
the bottom while you lift.
Otherwise, put a heavy rock at
the base to keep it from sliding
while lifting.

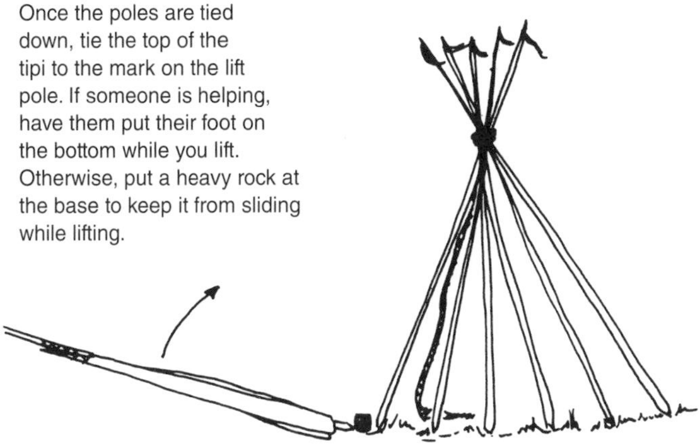

After the 14 poles are pitched,
take the rope and wrap around
about 3 times, bring through and
tie down tightly.

Cross stakes for
tying tipi down.

Setting Up the Tipi
(continued)

For the ties on the cover, insert a round rock and tie nylon cord around leaving plenty for twisting rope and tying down on the stake.

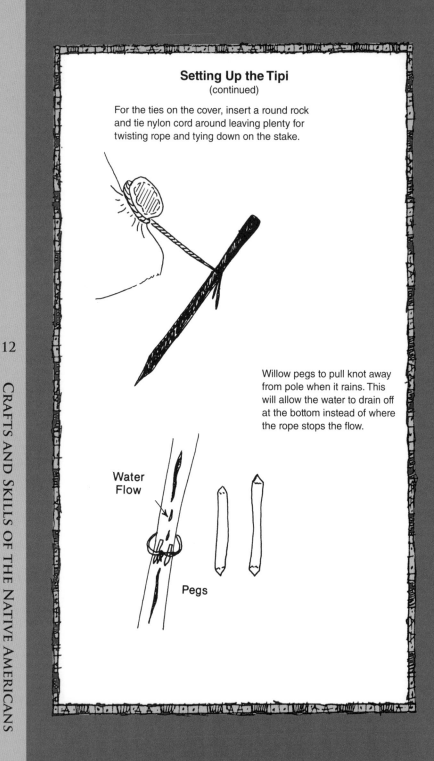

Willow pegs to pull knot away from pole when it rains. This will allow the water to drain off at the bottom instead of where the rope stops the flow.

Water Flow

Pegs

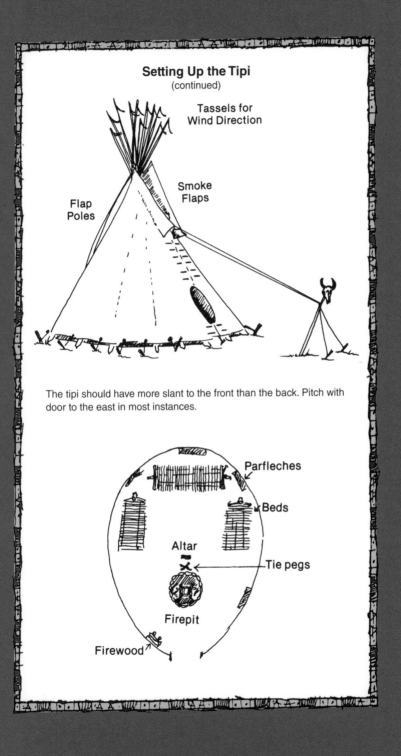

Setting Up the Tipi
(continued)

Tassels for Wind Direction

Smoke Flaps

Flap Poles

The tipi should have more slant to the front than the back. Pitch with door to the east in most instances.

Parfleches

Beds

Altar

Tie pegs

Firepit

Firewood

13

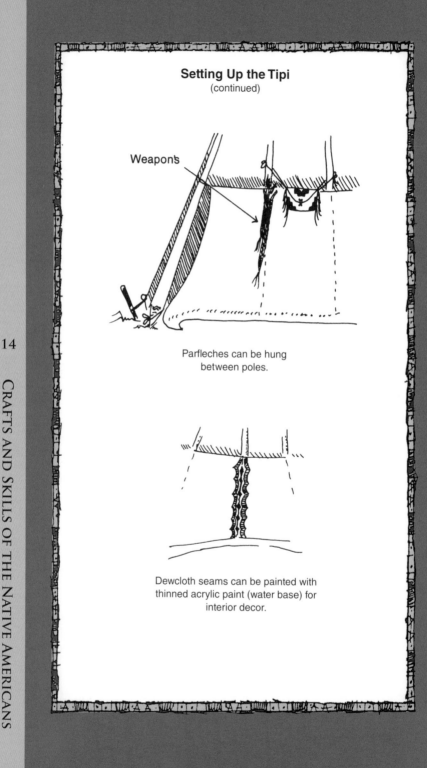

Setting Up the Tipi
(continued)

Weapons

Parfleches can be hung
between poles.

Dewcloth seams can be painted with
thinned acrylic paint (water base) for
interior decor.

CRAFTS AND SKILLS OF THE NATIVE AMERICANS

Ozan

The ozan acts as an inner roof and will help retain heat, plus give you some privacy when wanted.

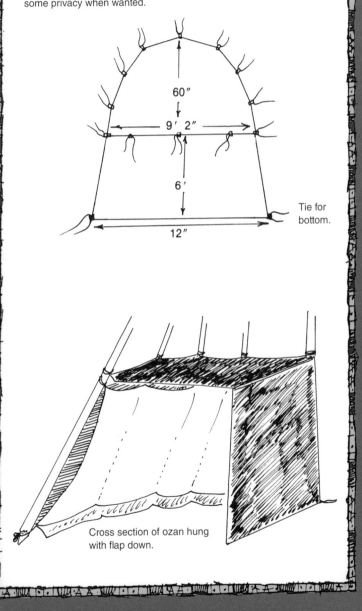

60"

9' 2"

6'

Tie for bottom.

12"

Cross section of ozan hung with flap down.

Tipi Fire Pit

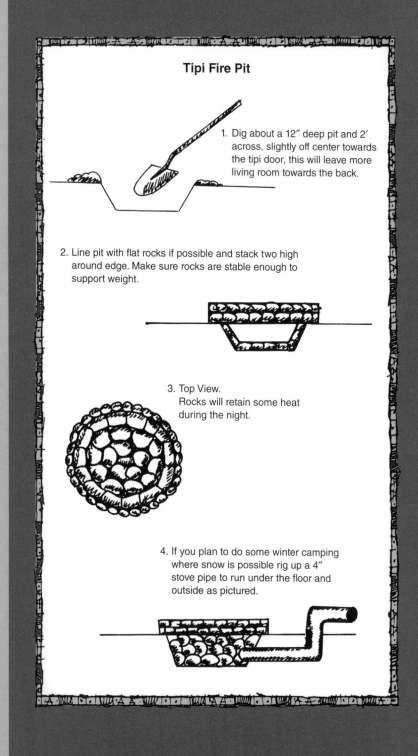

1. Dig about a 12″ deep pit and 2′ across, slightly off center towards the tipi door, this will leave more living room towards the back.

2. Line pit with flat rocks if possible and stack two high around edge. Make sure rocks are stable enough to support weight.

3. Top View.
   Rocks will retain some heat during the night.

4. If you plan to do some winter camping where snow is possible rig up a 4″ stove pipe to run under the floor and outside as pictured.

Tipi Pole Racks

Rack for Van

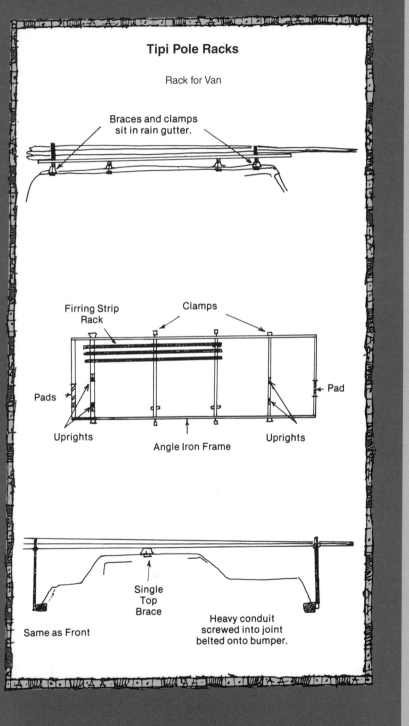

Braces and clamps sit in rain gutter.

Firring Strip Rack

Clamps

Pads

Pad

Uprights

Angle Iron Frame

Uprights

Same as Front

Single Top Brace

Heavy conduit screwed into joint belted onto bumper.

Stripping Poles

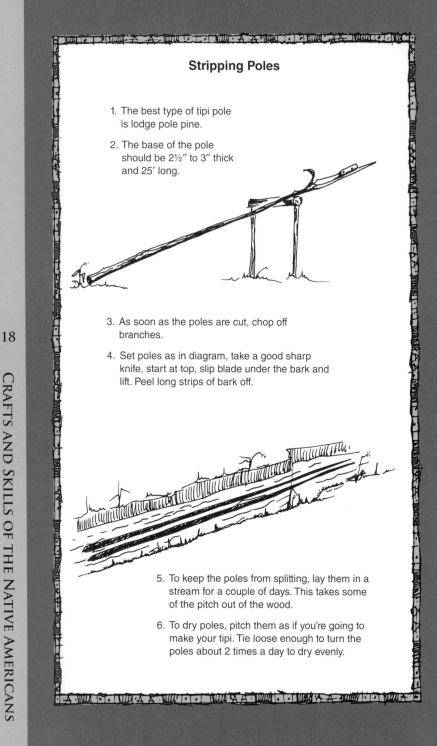

1. The best type of tipi pole is lodge pole pine.

2. The base of the pole should be 2½" to 3" thick and 25' long.

3. As soon as the poles are cut, chop off branches.

4. Set poles as in diagram, take a good sharp knife, start at top, slip blade under the bark and lift. Peel long strips of bark off.

5. To keep the poles from splitting, lay them in a stream for a couple of days. This takes some of the pitch out of the wood.

6. To dry poles, pitch them as if you're going to make your tipi. Tie loose enough to turn the poles about 2 times a day to dry evenly.

Painting the Tipi

Most lodges were not painted but, when they were, they were generally done by a specialist with the help of others. The symbols that were painted on the covers were to represent great feats, dreams, and protection as well as designating the family that owned the lodge. Having associated with various Native Americans, I have found that what was painted on a specific tipi was for that owner and no one else. In other words, no two tipis were painted the same. I would suggest, if you want to paint your tipi, that you honor those who have had theirs painted and published in books. Don't copy them. Create your own design to best represent what you feel needs to be portrayed.

The Wigwam

In the northern parts of the United States and across Canada, the Algonkian built their dome-shaped wigwam with saplings and covered birch bark, rushes, woven mats, or other forms of covering.

Saplings were bent and lashed together to form a sturdy framework. The ends were stuck in the ground for stability. Bark was cut in sections large enough to be sewn across each cross-brace on the top with enough overhang to overlap the top portion of bark sewn on below. The only light sources were a door on one end and a smoke hole in the top. The fire was built in the middle of the wigwam with rushes or grasses for floor covering. Beds were elevated off the damp ground.

These wigwams were very stable dwellings. They could be lived in for quite a long time. Today it would be more feasible to use canvas for the covering since the amount of bark to be used would kill trees from which the bark was taken.

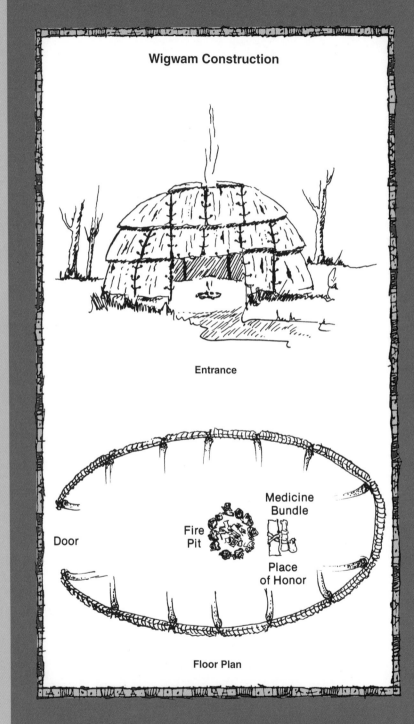

Wigwam Construction

Entrance

Floor Plan

Door

Fire Pit

Medicine Bundle

Place of Honor

Wigwam Construction
(continued)

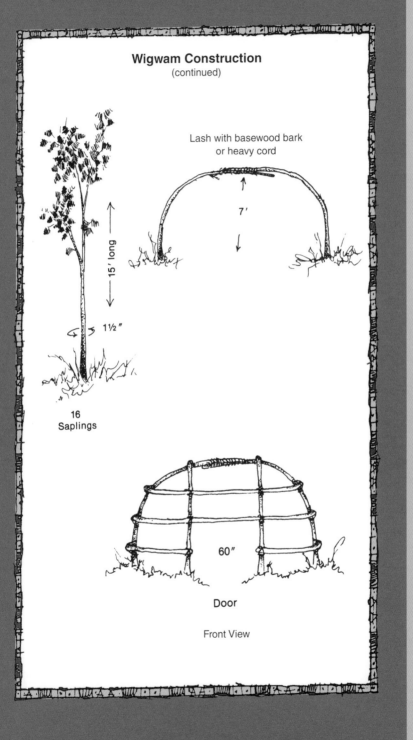

Lash with basewood bark
or heavy cord

7'

15' long

1½"

16
Saplings

60"

Door

Front View

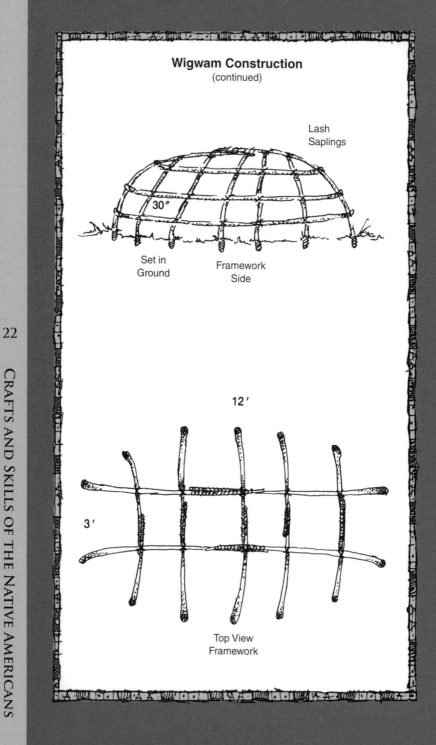

Wigwam Construction

(continued)

Lash
Saplings

30"

Set in
Ground

Framework
Side

12'

3'

Top View
Framework

Wigwam Construction
(continued)

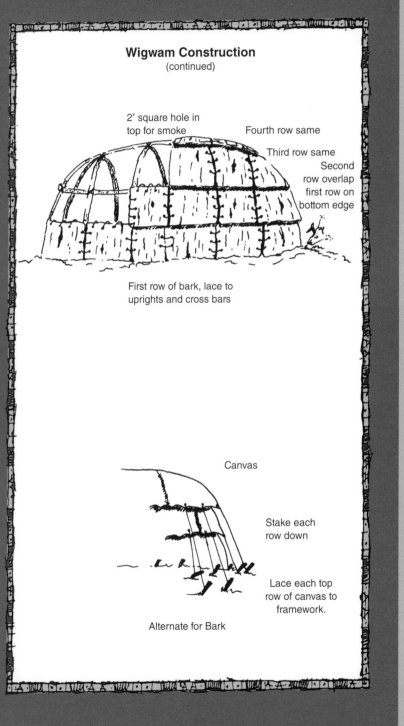

2' square hole in top for smoke

Fourth row same

Third row same

Second row overlap first row on bottom edge

First row of bark, lace to uprights and cross bars

Canvas

Stake each row down

Lace each top row of canvas to framework.

Alternate for Bark

The Pit Dwelling

This dwelling was used by such tribes as the Patwin, Mandan, Mogollon, Fremont, and Eskimo although the dwellings varied in size and shape. Some were large enough to house the owner's horses. This is a dwelling that can be lived in year round. It is quite comfortable in either winter or summer. Cedar poles are sometimes available at lumber companies in the western states, but you need to make sure the poles are forked at the top and broad at the base. The center pole should be at least 12 inches across. If you have the property and want a permanent structure to live in or for a place to have club meetings that would be most unique, this may be the structure you will want.

Pit House Construction

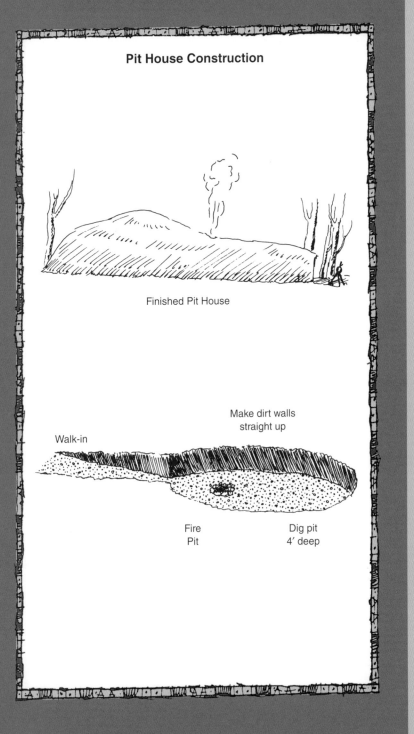

Finished Pit House

Make dirt walls
straight up

Walk-in

Fire
Pit

Dig pit
4′ deep

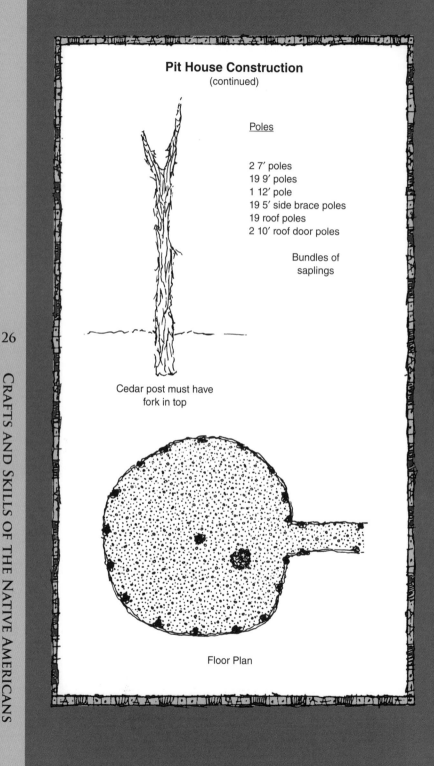

Pit House Construction
(continued)

<u>Poles</u>

2 7' poles
19 9' poles
1 12' pole
19 5' side brace poles
19 roof poles
2 10' roof door poles

Bundles of
saplings

Cedar post must have
fork in top

Floor Plan

Pit House Construction
(continued)

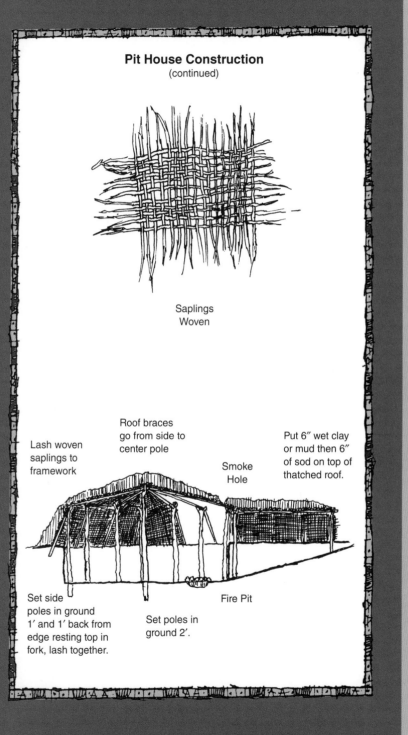

Saplings
Woven

Roof braces
go from side to
center pole

Lash woven
saplings to
framework

Put 6″ wet clay
or mud then 6″
of sod on top of
thatched roof.

Smoke
Hole

Set side
poles in ground
1′ and 1′ back from
edge resting top in
fork, lash together.

Set poles in
ground 2′.

Fire Pit

The type, style, and use of tools are many. Unlike weapons, tools were used to maintain everyday living, which included digging, grinding, pounding, cutting, scraping, and punching holes rather than as implements to take a life of either man or beast.

Tools were made of stone so hard that they were used to peck, grind, sharpen, and polish other stone and other materials such as wood, antler, horn, and bone. Drill heads were sometimes made of basalt while scrapers might be made of obsidian, which was sharper than surgical scalpels. Wood was used for bow-drill fires as well as drills and root diggers, and as handles for many other tools. Antler and bone were turned into needles, pins, weaving tools, awls, fish hooks, musical instruments, spoons and knife handles. Steel, when it was introduced, was used for many of these items.

The tools here are of such a nature as to allow you to make your choice of which would serve you best for the occasion. Stone, bone, wood, and steel can usually be found in your area and, with little trouble, some nice tools can be constructed.

CHAPTER 2
TOOLS

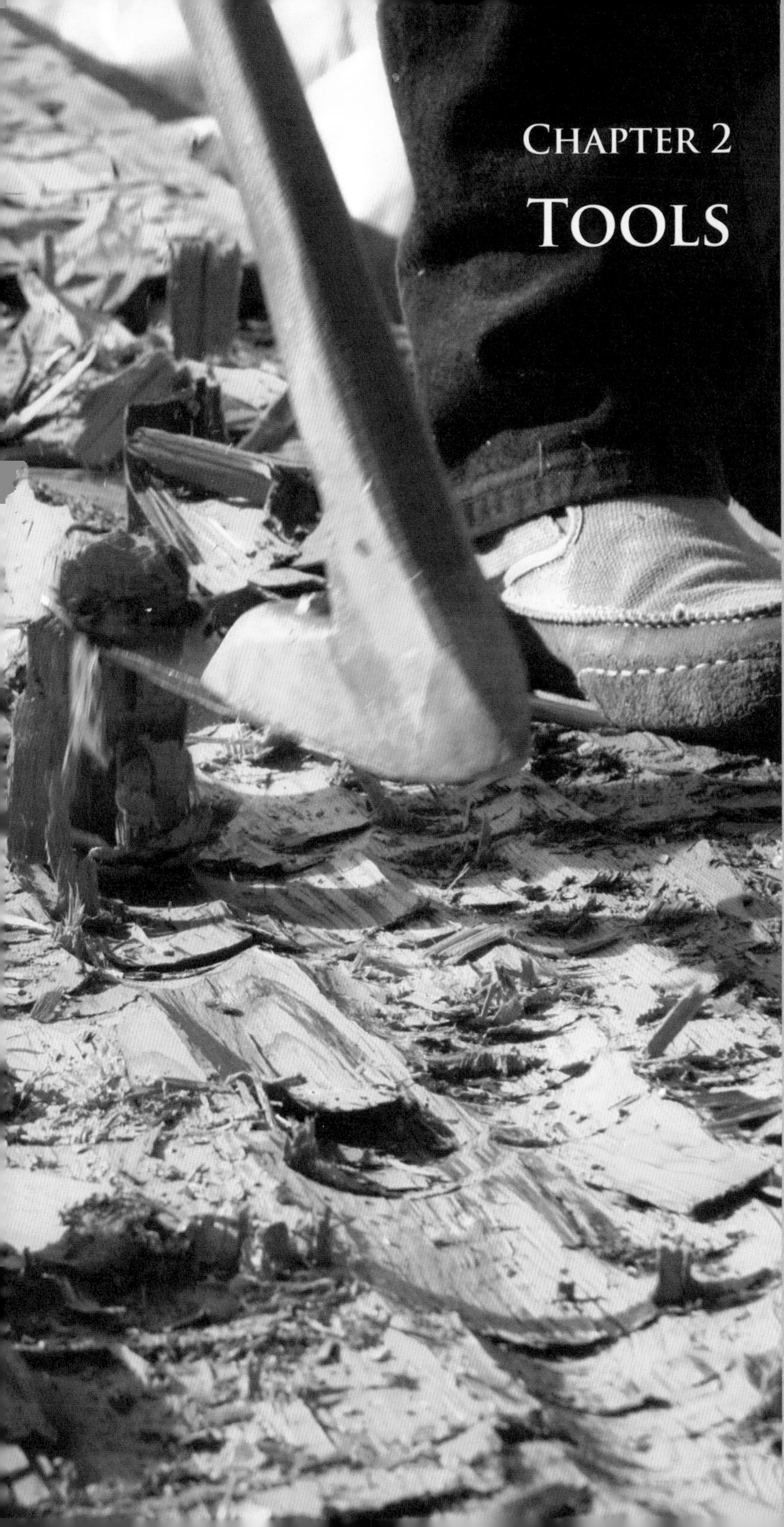

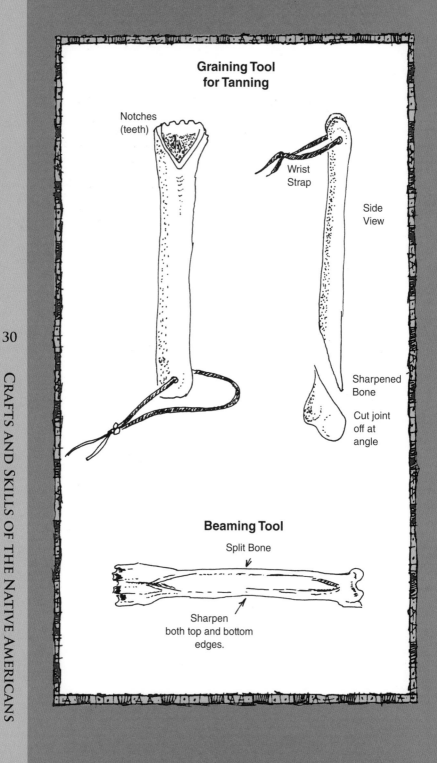

**Graining Tool
for Tanning**

Notches
(teeth)

Wrist
Strap

Side
View

Sharpened
Bone

Cut joint
off at
angle

Beaming Tool

Split Bone

Sharpen
both top and bottom
edges.

CRAFTS AND SKILLS OF THE NATIVE AMERICANS

Firemaking

For bow drill method you will need:

1. Wood—cottonwood, sagebrush or white elm.

2. Green, curved stick for the bow with a fork on one end.

←——— @ 24" ———→

3. Leather cord, split one end as shown to insert plug.

@ 30" long

4. Handle for spindle to fit in the palm of your hand made of stone or hardwood.

5. Shredded bark of cottonwood, birch, cedar or sage for tinder.

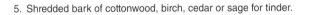

6. Bark slab to catch the spark.

7. Spindle of yucca, cottonwood or other mentioned wood.

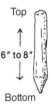

Top

↑
6" to 8"
↓

Bottom

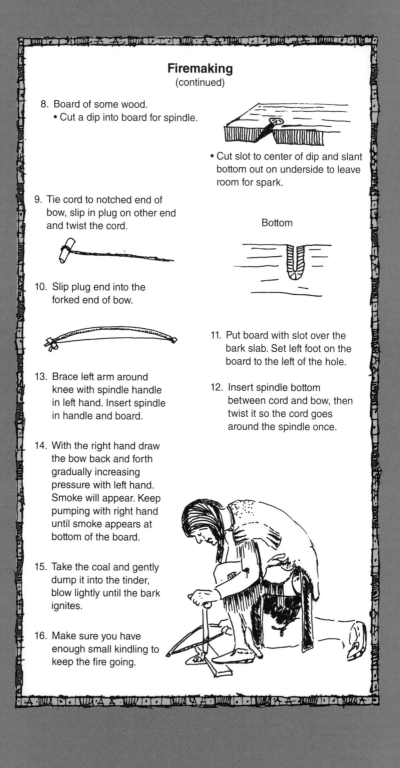

Firemaking
(continued)

8. Board of some wood.
   • Cut a dip into board for spindle.

   • Cut slot to center of dip and slant bottom out on underside to leave room for spark.

9. Tie cord to notched end of bow, slip in plug on other end and twist the cord.

Bottom

10. Slip plug end into the forked end of bow.

11. Put board with slot over the bark slab. Set left foot on the board to the left of the hole.

12. Insert spindle bottom between cord and bow, then twist it so the cord goes around the spindle once.

13. Brace left arm around knee with spindle handle in left hand. Insert spindle in handle and board.

14. With the right hand draw the bow back and forth gradually increasing pressure with left hand. Smoke will appear. Keep pumping with right hand until smoke appears at bottom of the board.

15. Take the coal and gently dump it into the tinder, blow lightly until the bark ignites.

16. Make sure you have enough small kindling to keep the fire going.

CRAFTS AND SKILLS OF THE NATIVE AMERICANS

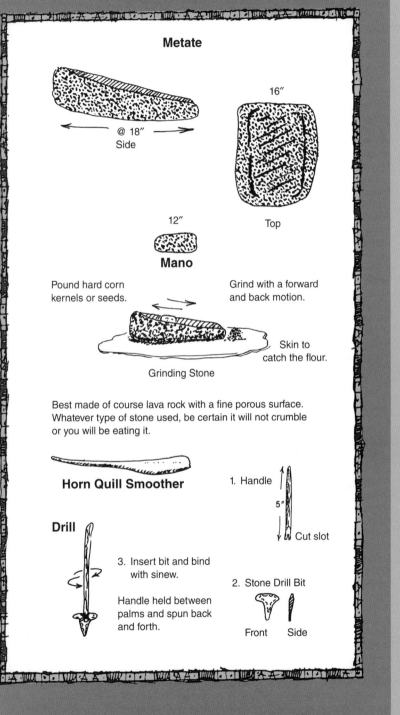

Metate

@ 18"
Side

16"

Top

12"

Mano

Pound hard corn
kernels or seeds.

Grind with a forward
and back motion.

Skin to
catch the flour.

Grinding Stone

Best made of course lava rock with a fine porous surface.
Whatever type of stone used, be certain it will not crumble
or you will be eating it.

Horn Quill Smoother

1. Handle

5"

Cut slot

Drill

3. Insert bit and bind
   with sinew.

Handle held between
palms and spun back
and forth.

2. Stone Drill Bit

Front   Side

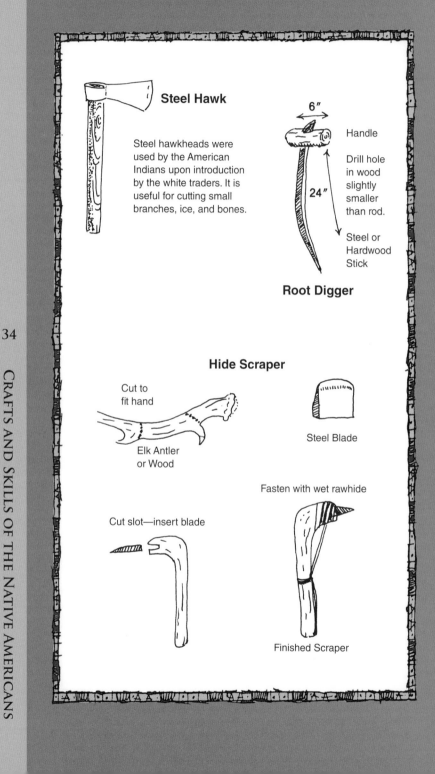

Steel Hawk

Steel hawkheads were used by the American Indians upon introduction by the white traders. It is useful for cutting small branches, ice, and bones.

6″

Handle

Drill hole in wood slightly smaller than rod.

24″

Steel or Hardwood Stick

Root Digger

Hide Scraper

Cut to fit hand

Elk Antler or Wood

Steel Blade

Cut slot—insert blade

Fasten with wet rawhide

Finished Scraper

Hammer Stone

Pecking stone to make notch around stone for either finger grip or handle.

Grind on sandstone to refine shape.

Polish with leather pulling back and forth.

Front   Side

TOOLS

Hammer Stone
(continued)

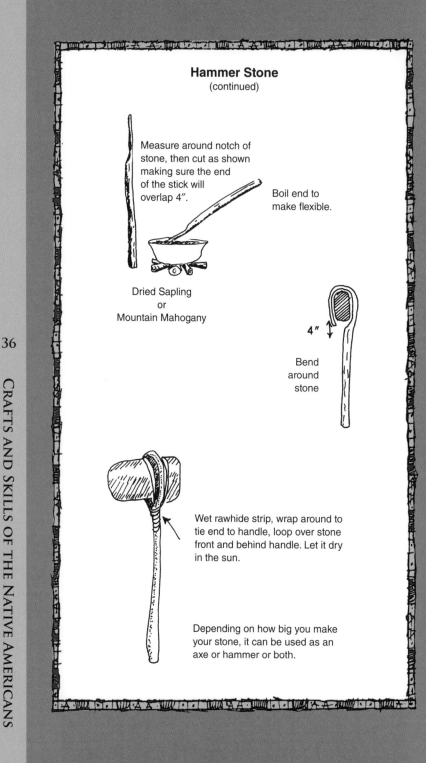

Measure around notch of stone, then cut as shown making sure the end of the stick will overlap 4″.

Boil end to make flexible.

Dried Sapling
or
Mountain Mahogany

4″

Bend around stone

Wet rawhide strip, wrap around to tie end to handle, loop over stone front and behind handle. Let it dry in the sun.

Depending on how big you make your stone, it can be used as an axe or hammer or both.

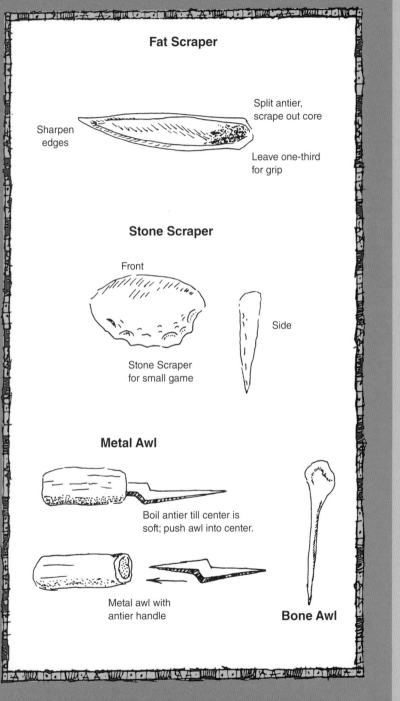

Fat Scraper

Split antier,
scrape out core

Sharpen
edges

Leave one-third
for grip

Stone Scraper

Front

Side

Stone Scraper
for small game

Metal Awl

Boil antier till center is
soft; push awl into center.

Metal awl with
antier handle

Bone Awl

The arsenal of the American Indian was mainly limited to stone, bone, and wooden implements before the coming of the white man. When explorers, traders, and trappers appeared, the American Indians made use of factory-made items when they could. Even after they obtained the gun and the metal hawk-head, they still used their traditional weapons of bow and arrow, lance and shield.

Knives made of stone though sharp and easy to make were brittle and virtually left the scene after the introduction of the steel knife. The same thing happened with the stone arrowhead.

Lances were wrapped with such furs as otter, mink, and beaver as well as bird feathers which represented certain meanings and powers to the individual warrior. Some of the meanings are: crow feathers because the crow was the first to find food; owl representing the north star; and swan feathers representing the thunderbird.

Bows were simply decorated, if at all, and made strictly for function as were the arrows. When points were used, the heads were loosely attached so that they would come off when pulled out of the victim.

The weapons in this chapter are selected to serve you as a hunting tool or a decorative piece.

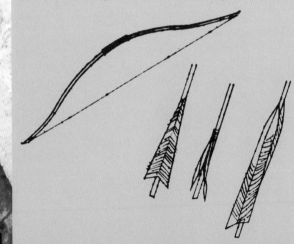

CHAPTER 3
WEAPONS

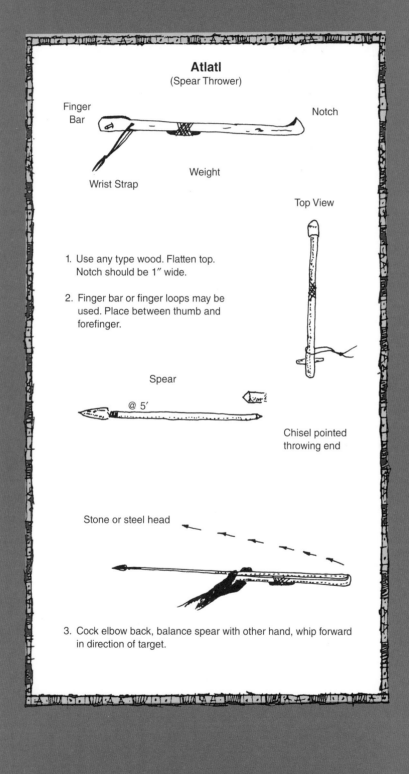

Atlatl
(Spear Thrower)

Finger Bar

Notch

Weight

Wrist Strap

Top View

1. Use any type wood. Flatten top. Notch should be 1″ wide.

2. Finger bar or finger loops may be used. Place between thumb and forefinger.

Spear

@ 5′

Chisel pointed throwing end

Stone or steel head

3. Cock elbow back, balance spear with other hand, whip forward in direction of target.

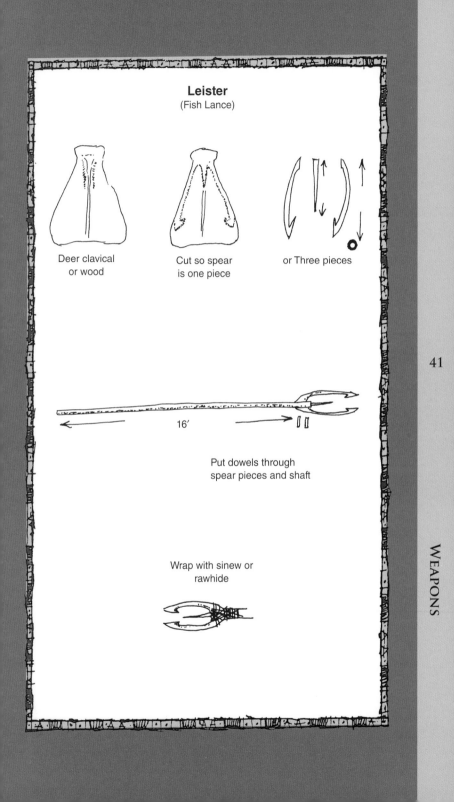

Leister
(Fish Lance)

Deer clavical
or wood

Cut so spear
is one piece

or Three pieces

16′

Put dowels through
spear pieces and shaft

Wrap with sinew or
rawhide

War Lance and Points

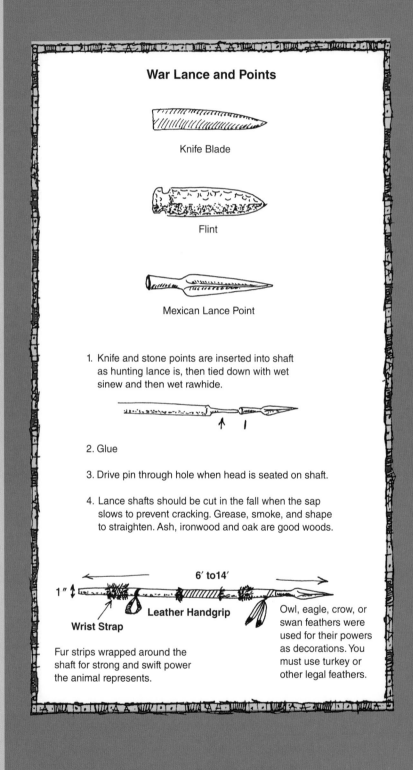

Knife Blade

Flint

Mexican Lance Point

1. Knife and stone points are inserted into shaft as hunting lance is, then tied down with wet sinew and then wet rawhide.

2. Glue

3. Drive pin through hole when head is seated on shaft.

4. Lance shafts should be cut in the fall when the sap slows to prevent cracking. Grease, smoke, and shape to straighten. Ash, ironwood and oak are good woods.

6′ to14′

1″

Leather Handgrip

Wrist Strap

Fur strips wrapped around the shaft for strong and swift power the animal represents.

Owl, eagle, crow, or swan feathers were used for their powers as decorations. You must use turkey or other legal feathers.

War Lance and Points
(continued)

Hunting Lance

1. Split leg bone of deer, elk, or other large bone.

10" to 12"

2. Cut out rough shape, scrape out marrow and form lance point.

3. Sharpen flat edge.

4. Hollow allows for bleeding animals.

5. Stone or metal points may be used.

6. Shaft should be about 2" in diameter, hard, polished wood.

7. Boil pine pitch and while hot insert bottom of point into pitch and quickly insert into shaft slot.

8. Wrap around slot with wet rawhide strip.

Hunting lances were only lightly decorated.

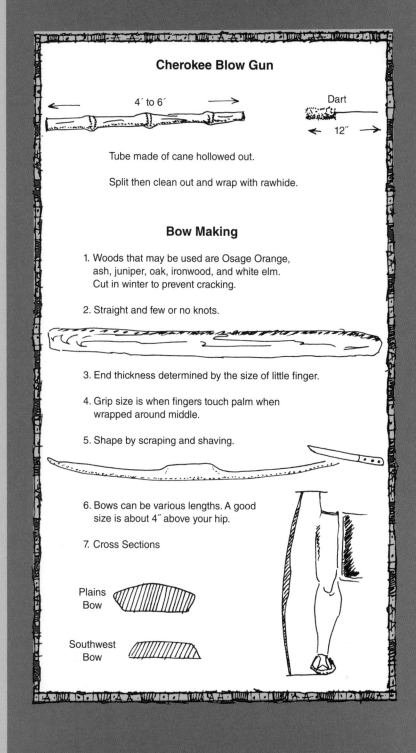

Cherokee Blow Gun

← 4′ to 6′ →

Dart

← 12″ →

Tube made of cane hollowed out.

Split then clean out and wrap with rawhide.

Bow Making

1. Woods that may be used are Osage Orange, ash, juniper, oak, ironwood, and white elm. Cut in winter to prevent cracking.

2. Straight and few or no knots.

3. End thickness determined by the size of little finger.

4. Grip size is when fingers touch palm when wrapped around middle.

5. Shape by scraping and shaving.

6. Bows can be various lengths. A good size is about 4″ above your hip.

7. Cross Sections

Plains Bow

Southwest Bow

Bow Making
(continued)

8. Once the bow is shaped, it is backed with sinew that has been dried, then pounded. It is glued with hoof and horn glue (LePages glue will work) in strips with layers of fine white clay between. Two layers are sufficient to reinforce the wood. Not all bows were backed.

9. Bows can be oiled, heated and shaped to help flexibility.

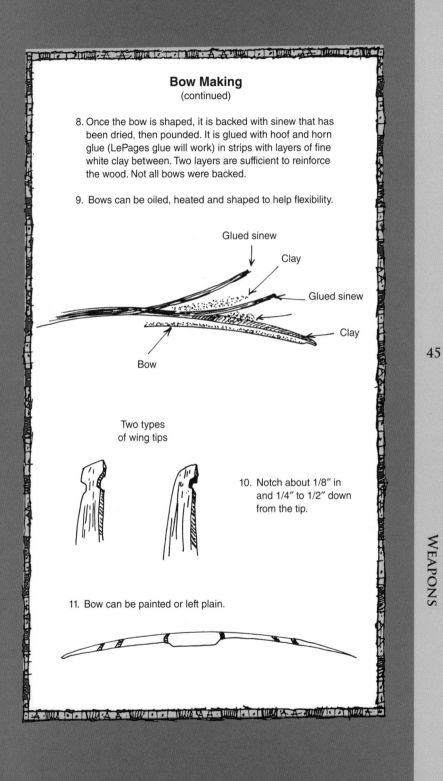

Glued sinew

Clay

Glued sinew

Clay

Bow

Two types
of wing tips

10. Notch about 1/8″ in and 1/4″ to 1/2″ down from the tip.

11. Bow can be painted or left plain.

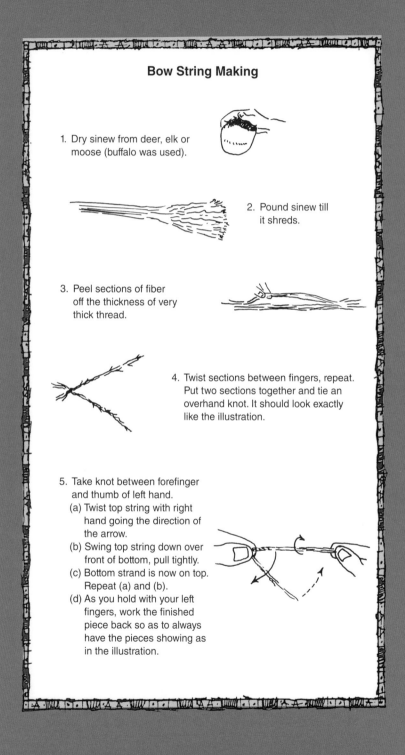

Bow String Making

1. Dry sinew from deer, elk or moose (buffalo was used).

2. Pound sinew till it shreds.

3. Peel sections of fiber off the thickness of very thick thread.

4. Twist sections between fingers, repeat. Put two sections together and tie an overhand knot. It should look exactly like the illustration.

5. Take knot between forefinger and thumb of left hand.
   (a) Twist top string with right hand going the direction of the arrow.
   (b) Swing top string down over front of bottom, pull tightly.
   (c) Bottom strand is now on top. Repeat (a) and (b).
   (d) As you hold with your left fingers, work the finished piece back so as to always have the pieces showing as in the illustration.

Bow String Making
(continued)

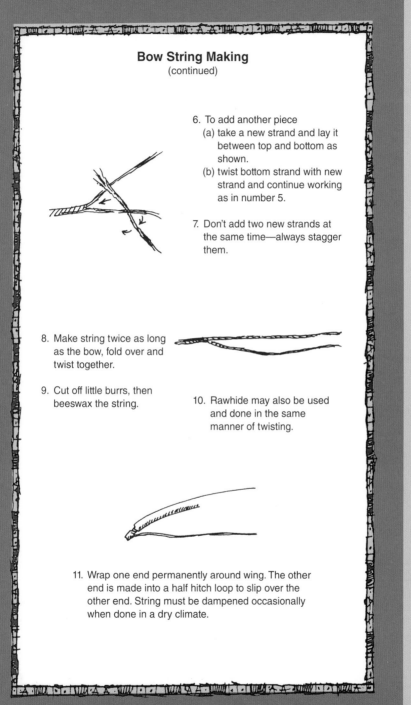

6. To add another piece
   (a) take a new strand and lay it between top and bottom as shown.
   (b) twist bottom strand with new strand and continue working as in number 5.

7. Don't add two new strands at the same time—always stagger them.

8. Make string twice as long as the bow, fold over and twist together.

9. Cut off little burrs, then beeswax the string.

10. Rawhide may also be used and done in the same manner of twisting.

11. Wrap one end permanently around wing. The other end is made into a half hitch loop to slip over the other end. String must be dampened occasionally when done in a dry climate.

47

WEAPONS

Arrows

The arrow can be made of many types of wood, birch, willow, cane, but it must be straight or you must be able to straighten the shaft. Make sure that the shaft is at least 28″ to start with.

1. Select wood for the shaft.

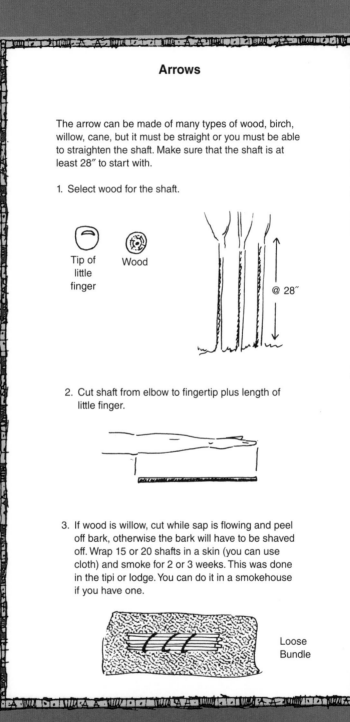

Tip of little finger

Wood

@ 28″

2. Cut shaft from elbow to fingertip plus length of little finger.

3. If wood is willow, cut while sap is flowing and peel off bark, otherwise the bark will have to be shaved off. Wrap 15 or 20 shafts in a skin (you can use cloth) and smoke for 2 or 3 weeks. This was done in the tipi or lodge. You can do it in a smokehouse if you have one.

Loose Bundle

Arrows
(continued)

4. Smoke Bundle

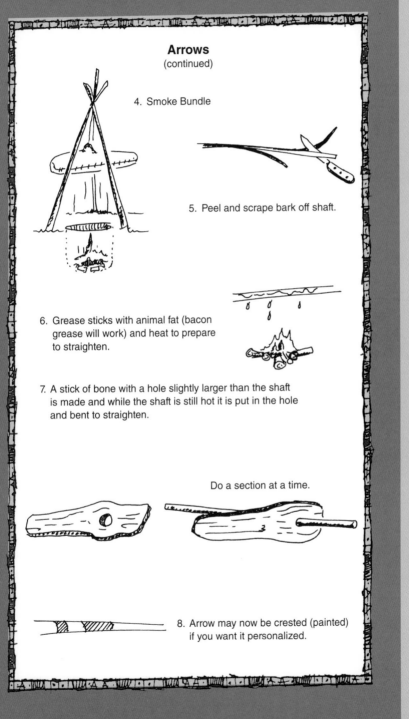

5. Peel and scrape bark off shaft.

6. Grease sticks with animal fat (bacon grease will work) and heat to prepare to straighten.

7. A stick of bone with a hole slightly larger than the shaft is made and while the shaft is still hot it is put in the hole and bent to straighten.

Do a section at a time.

8. Arrow may now be crested (painted) if you want it personalized.

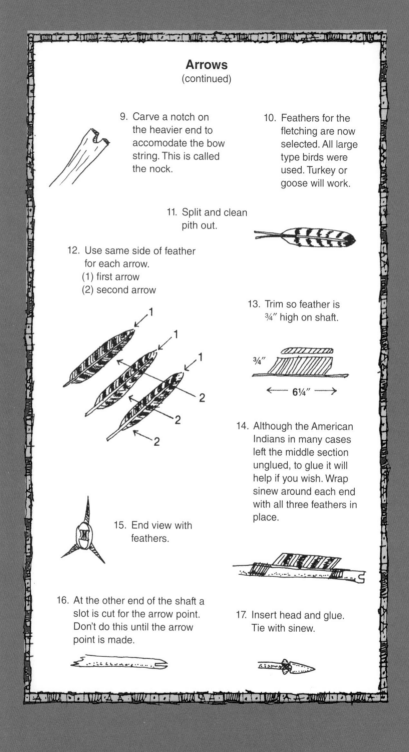

Arrows
(continued)

9. Carve a notch on the heavier end to accomodate the bow string. This is called the nock.

10. Feathers for the fletching are now selected. All large type birds were used. Turkey or goose will work.

11. Split and clean pith out.

12. Use same side of feather for each arrow.
   (1) first arrow
   (2) second arrow

13. Trim so feather is ¾" high on shaft.

¾"

←—— 6¼" ——→

14. Although the American Indians in many cases left the middle section unglued, to glue it will help if you wish. Wrap sinew around each end with all three feathers in place.

15. End view with feathers.

16. At the other end of the shaft a slot is cut for the arrow point. Don't do this until the arrow point is made.

17. Insert head and glue. Tie with sinew.

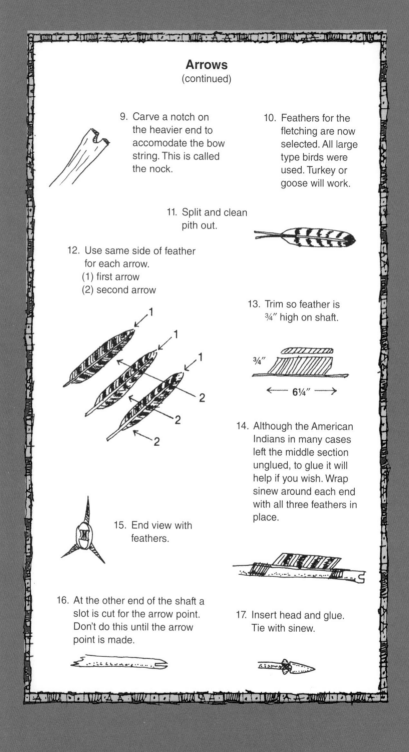

50

CRAFTS AND SKILLS OF THE NATIVE AMERICANS

Arrow Points

Arrow points can be made of steel, bone, or stone. Great Lakes tribes used copper as far back as 1500 B.C.

1. Types of stone:
   agate
   flint
   slate
   obsidian

2. Tools:
   billet from elk
   deer antler tip for pressure flaking
   leather pad

3. Hammer stone.

   Nodule

   Spall

   Making flakes

4. Start forming by hitting spall to thin point as shown. Continue forming basic shape.

6. Finished point.

5. Put pad in hand. Grip spall and begin chipping with antler applying pressure down and out.

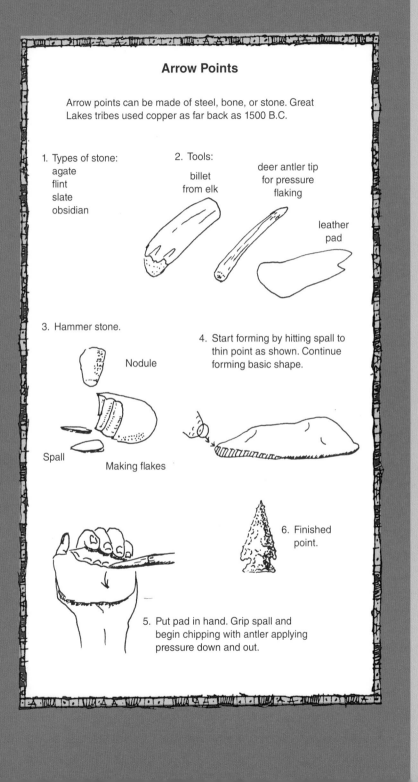

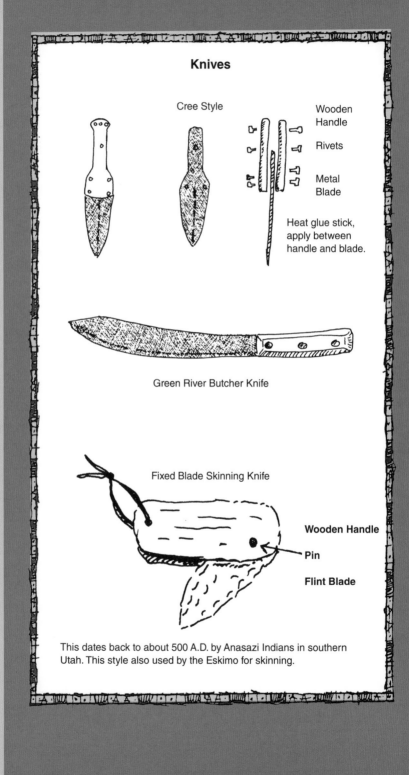

Knives

Cree Style

Wooden Handle

Rivets

Metal Blade

Heat glue stick, apply between handle and blade.

Green River Butcher Knife

Fixed Blade Skinning Knife

Wooden Handle

Pin

Flint Blade

This dates back to about 500 A.D. by Anasazi Indians in southern Utah. This style also used by the Eskimo for skinning.

In order for the American Indian to survive, it was of utmost importance for the male child to be trained early to understand the habits of animals and their use to man. Everything from buffalo to grasshoppers were sought after and eaten. They lived where the land could provide them with the particular diet they were used to such as fish from the Columbia River, grasshoppers and ants on the desert, buffalo on the plains, beaver in Canada, and vegetables, wild turkey and deer in the woodlands.

Today you must know your state laws on hunting, fishing, and trapping. Proclamations can be obtained from your Division of Wildlife Resources. Know the laws and follow them diligently for your protection and to help maintain a balanced wildlife.

To learn hunting as the Native Americans hunted, takes time and patience. You must know what animal you are after, find out what the habits of the animal are, find where it lives, what it eats, and when. After you are thoroughly familiar with the animal you must learn to cover your scent and wait for the animal to come to you or be prepared to take a long, quiet hike hoping to find traces of the animal you are hunting.

Buffalo were not always hunted from horseback. Sometimes they were driven into stockades or over a cliff when the terrain permitted. Today special permits are drawn for hunts and in some areas they are much harder to find and hunt than in olden times.

Game birds were either trapped by deadfall or with nets. The larger eastern turkey was shot.

Spear fishing was done on major waterways and lakes. Fishline made of Indian hemp or sinew and bone or wooden hooks were also used.

CHAPTER 4

HUNTING, TRACKING, AND TRAPPING

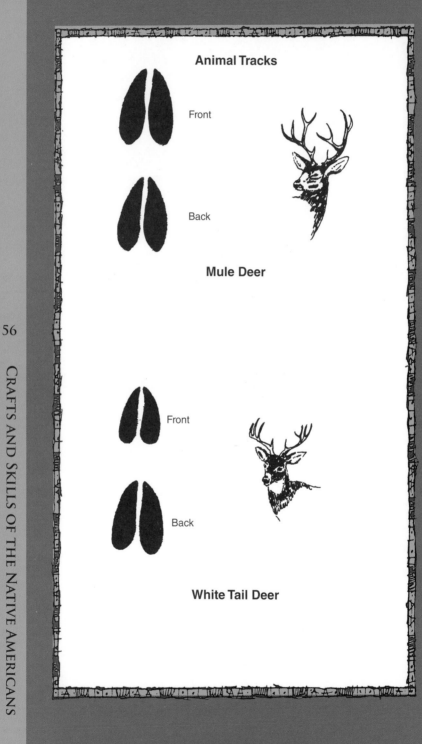

Animal Tracks

Front

Back

Mule Deer

Front

Back

White Tail Deer

CRAFTS AND SKILLS OF THE NATIVE AMERICANS

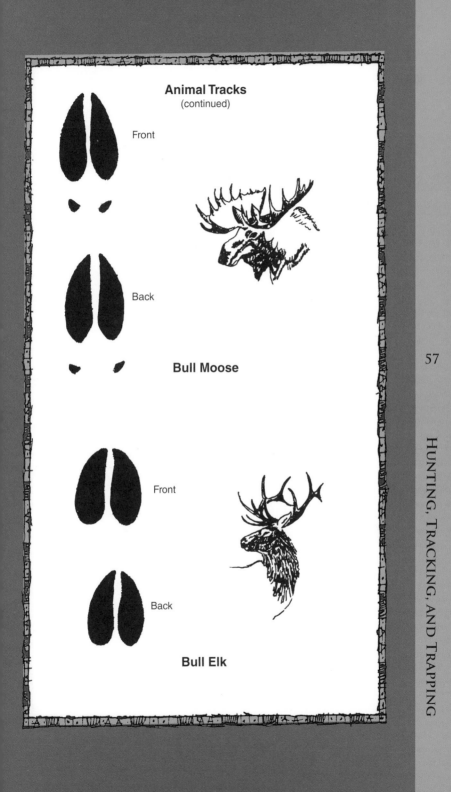

Animal Tracks
(continued)

Front

Back

Bull Moose

Front

Back

Bull Elk

HUNTING, TRACKING, AND TRAPPING

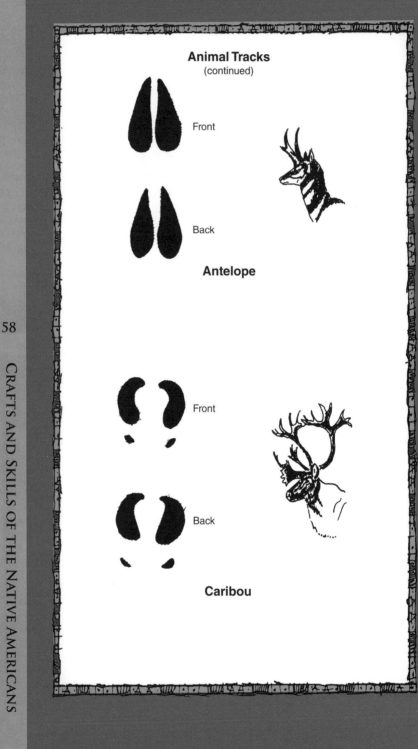

Animal Tracks
(continued)

Front

Back

Antelope

Front

Back

Caribou

CRAFTS AND SKILLS OF THE NATIVE AMERICANS

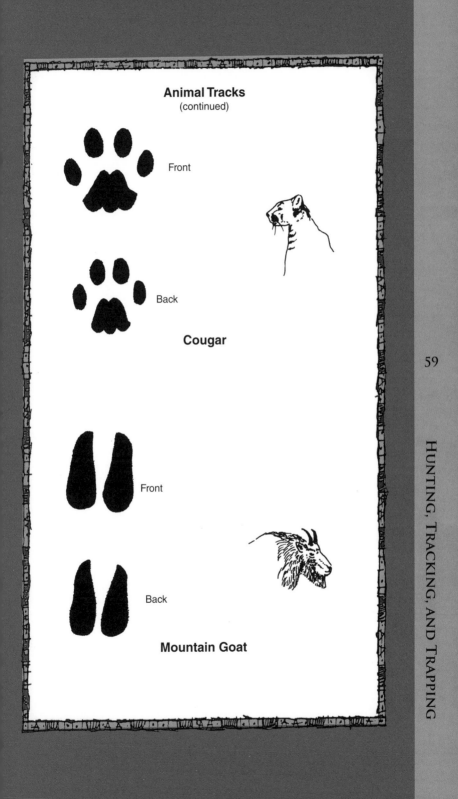

Animal Tracks
(continued)

Front

Back

Cougar

Front

Back

Mountain Goat

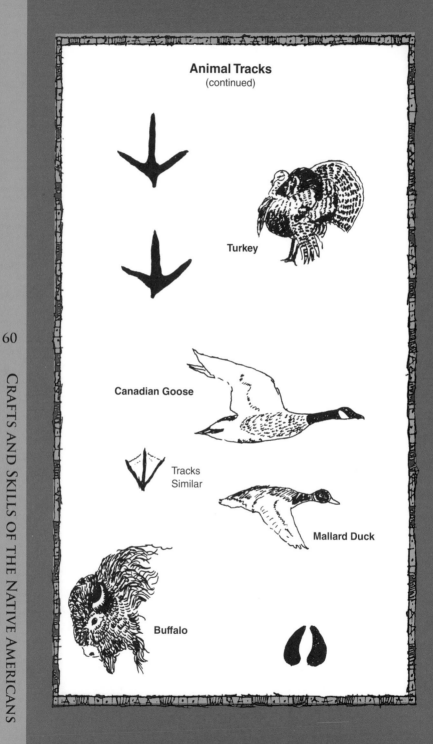

Animal Tracks
(continued)

Turkey

Canadian Goose

Tracks
Similar

Mallard Duck

Buffalo

CRAFTS AND SKILLS OF THE NATIVE AMERICANS

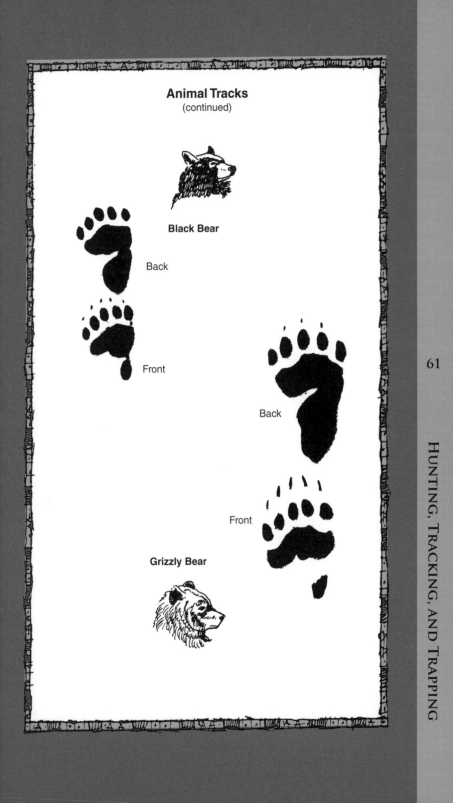

Animal Tracks
(continued)

Black Bear

Back

Front

Back

Front

Grizzly Bear

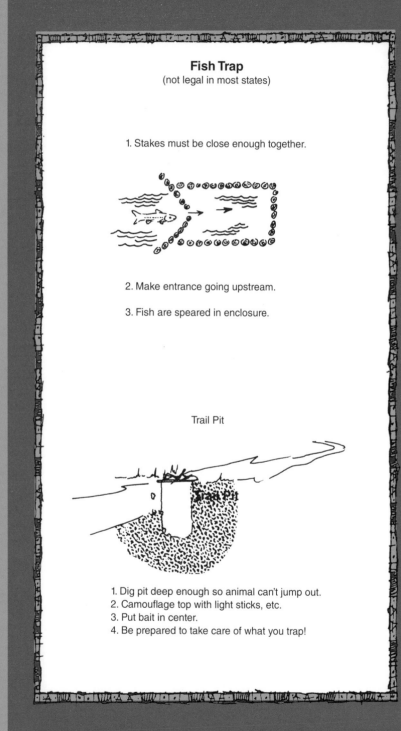

Fish Trap
(not legal in most states)

1. Stakes must be close enough together.

2. Make entrance going upstream.

3. Fish are speared in enclosure.

Trail Pit

1. Dig pit deep enough so animal can't jump out.
2. Camouflage top with light sticks, etc.
3. Put bait in center.
4. Be prepared to take care of what you trap!

Snare Trap

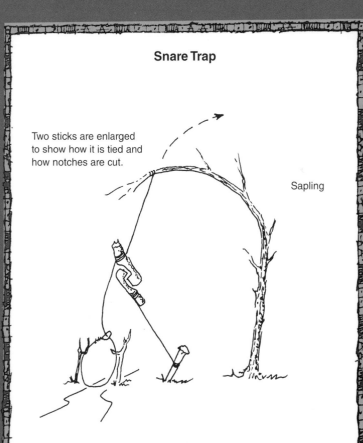

Two sticks are enlarged to show how it is tied and how notches are cut.

Sapling

1. Cut twine or wire in 3 desired lengths.
2. Cut two small sticks (willow works great) and make notches as shown.
3. Tie noose to upper catch right above notch and to tip of sapling.
4. Tie lower catch tight below notch and stake down.
5. Bend sapling, hook upper and lower catch.
6. Set noose large enough for head to get through.

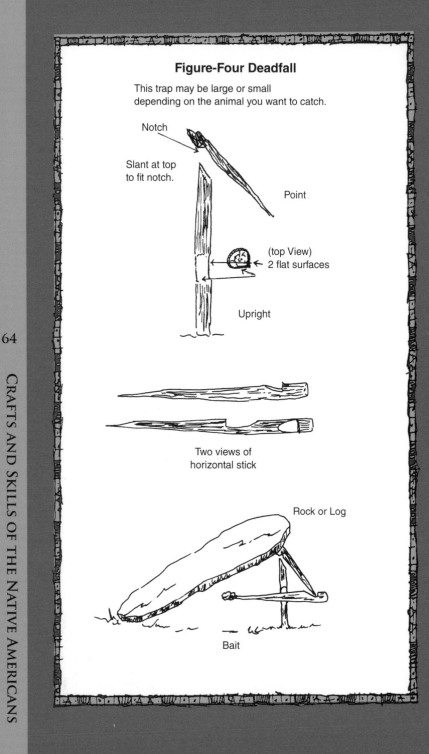

Figure-Four Deadfall

This trap may be large or small
depending on the animal you want to catch.

Notch

Slant at top
to fit notch.

Point

(top View)
2 flat surfaces

Upright

Two views of
horizontal stick

Rock or Log

Bait

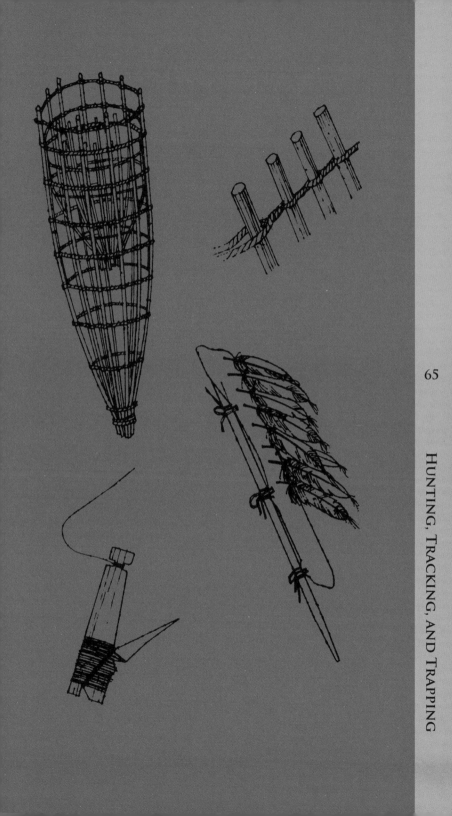

HUNTING, TRACKING, AND TRAPPING

M any a time I have had someone come up to me to ask if my squaw chewed the hide to tan it. Common sense and research has revealed to me that the closest a squaw came to chewing a hide was to soften the sinew to separate the strands or chewing a piece of already tanned hide to make a crease. The only tanning process that will be treated here is the one used by most tribes: brain tanning.

This will involve obtaining either the brain of the animal killed or getting some from your local butcher. When the process is completed, and done correctly, the beauty of the hide cannot be beaten. You can leave it white for ceremonial wear, and be very careful with it, or you can smoke it to the degree that it will be dark but soften up after becoming wet. Both sides will be like a fluffy suede.

CHAPTER 5
TANNING

Fleshing

1. Take hide with hair on, lay it over a smooth log with one end tucked between log and tree so hide won't slide.
2. Using a bone or steel fleshing tool, pull down scraping all membrane and fat off.
3. Hide may also be staked on the ground and fleshed.

Hair Removal

1. Putrifying—Hide is put in water, stirred frequently until hair slips (very smelly).

2. Lye and Water—2 cups full of hardwood ashes and water in a barrel (plastic). Add hide, stir until hair slips. This causes the hide to be gray in appearance.

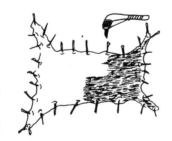

3. Stream Bed (not always available)—should have a rocky bottom with as little sand as possible. Put a heavy rock on one end and leave it until the hair is off.

4. Scraping—Stretch hide on ground with stakes. Make sure there are no rocks or lumps under it. Scrape starting at the neck and working down.

Braining

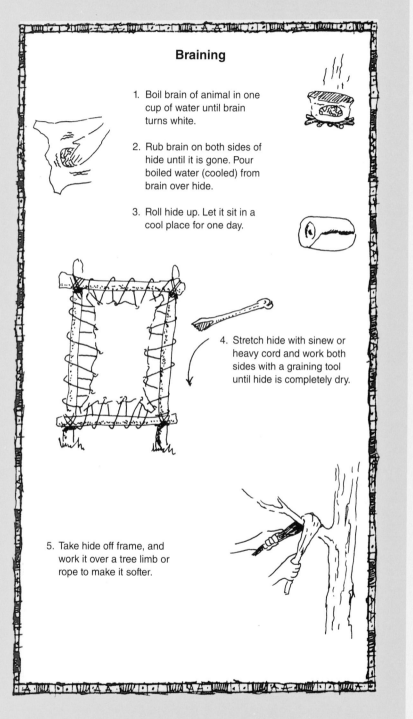

1. Boil brain of animal in one cup of water until brain turns white.

2. Rub brain on both sides of hide until it is gone. Pour boiled water (cooled) from brain over hide.

3. Roll hide up. Let it sit in a cool place for one day.

4. Stretch hide with sinew or heavy cord and work both sides with a graining tool until hide is completely dry.

5. Take hide off frame, and work it over a tree limb or rope to make it softer.

Smoking
(waterproofing)

1. Dig a pit 2′ deep and 1′ wide. Fill it with rotten wood and burn until there is no flame. Dampening wood will help create smoldering.
2. Sew hide together to make a cone with one open end.
3. Place hide over hole and hook it to a tripod staking it around the bottom of the hide.
4. The longer you smoke the hide the more waterproof it will be. This can be done for hours or days.
5. Do both sides.
6. Hide is now ready for use.

Rawhide

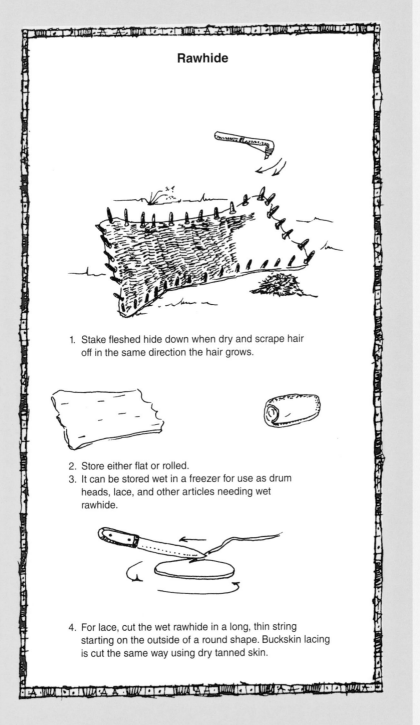

1. Stake fleshed hide down when dry and scrape hair off in the same direction the hair grows.

2. Store either flat or rolled.
3. It can be stored wet in a freezer for use as drum heads, lace, and other articles needing wet rawhide.

4. For lace, cut the wet rawhide in a long, thin string starting on the outside of a round shape. Buckskin lacing is cut the same way using dry tanned skin.

It is interesting to note that Native American fashion designers in the Americas were creating stylish clothing as far back as the Native American can be dated. Not all "savages" ran around without clothes on. Caribou, rabbit, deerskin, cotton, bark, and other materials were used for their attire. Of course, the climate and terrain had a lot to do with what they wore. This chapter will deal with the more common Plains Indian leggings and dresses that can be worn on most occasions.

Headgear consisted of furs, baskets, feathers, etc. In the movies you've seen the Native American with full-double trains on their headdresses going to battle looking so handsome. Yet imagine, with feathers flying in the wind, trying to get an arrow out of a quiver and getting all tangled up in the process. These works of art were used for ceremonial and special occasions and stored in a parfleche container when not in use.

Chapter 6
Clothing

Calico Shirt

In 1834 the Creeks, Seminoles, Sac and Fox were wearing calico shirts with or without collars. They were drop-sleeve without cuffs.

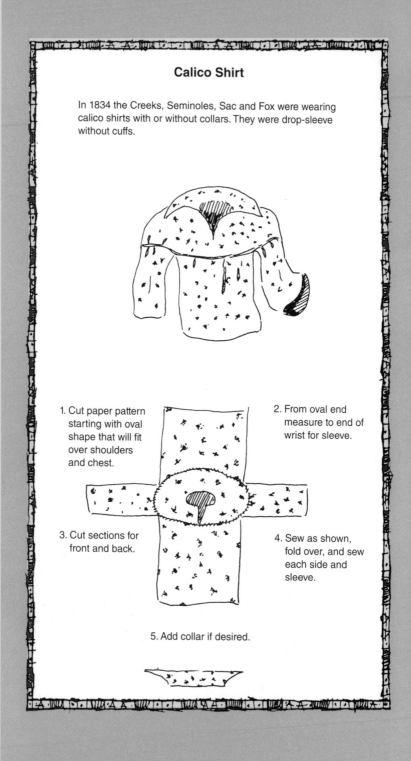

1. Cut paper pattern starting with oval shape that will fit over shoulders and chest.

2. From oval end measure to end of wrist for sleeve.

3. Cut sections for front and back.

4. Sew as shown, fold over, and sew each side and sleeve.

5. Add collar if desired.

Early Buckskin Shirt

The earliest buckskin shirts were very simple. A large buckskin hide was folded over and cut as shown below.

1. Cut

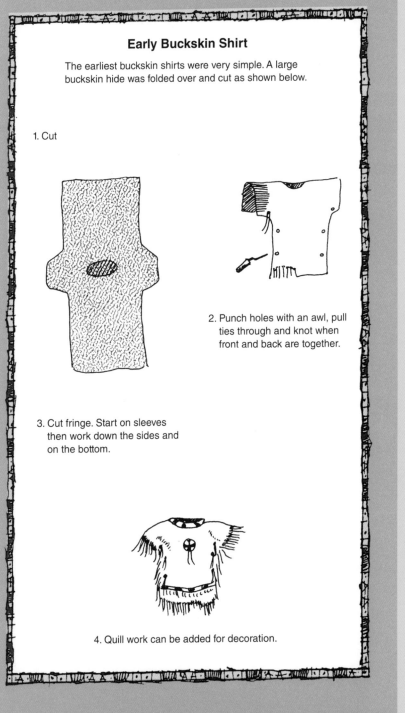

2. Punch holes with an awl, pull ties through and knot when front and back are together.

3. Cut fringe. Start on sleeves then work down the sides and on the bottom.

4. Quill work can be added for decoration.

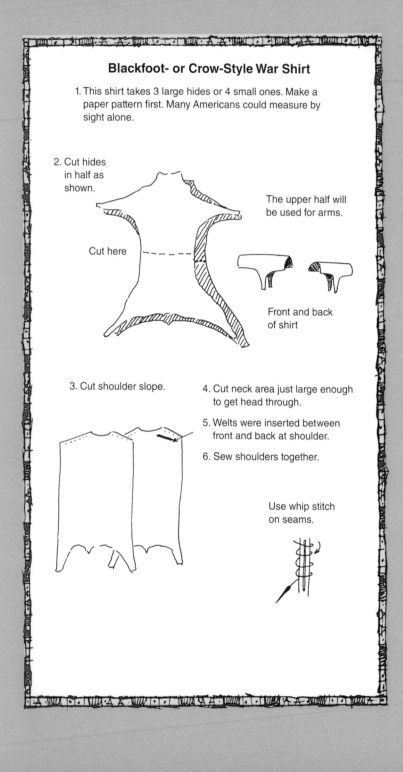

Blackfoot- or Crow-Style War Shirt

1. This shirt takes 3 large hides or 4 small ones. Make a paper pattern first. Many Americans could measure by sight alone.

2. Cut hides in half as shown.

The upper half will be used for arms.

Cut here

Front and back of shirt

3. Cut shoulder slope.

4. Cut neck area just large enough to get head through.

5. Welts were inserted between front and back at shoulder.

6. Sew shoulders together.

Use whip stitch on seams.

War Shirt
(continued)

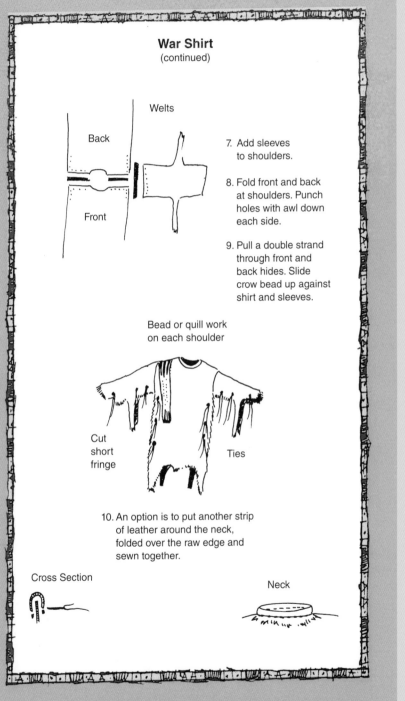

Welts

Back

Front

7. Add sleeves to shoulders.

8. Fold front and back at shoulders. Punch holes with awl down each side.

9. Pull a double strand through front and back hides. Slide crow bead up against shirt and sleeves.

Bead or quill work on each shoulder

Cut short fringe

Ties

10. An option is to put another strip of leather around the neck, folded over the raw edge and sewn together.

Cross Section

Neck

Buckskin Leggings

Leggings were very similar across the country with some variation in style.

1. Two hides are needed.

2. Lay hide neck down and cut the front legs off. Wrap skin around your leg and mark where they meet.

Early Sioux or Crow Style

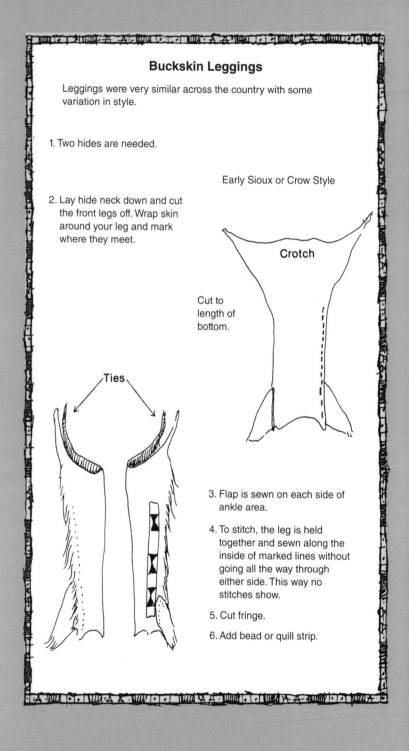

Crotch

Cut to length of bottom.

Ties

3. Flap is sewn on each side of ankle area.

4. To stitch, the leg is held together and sewn along the inside of marked lines without going all the way through either side. This way no stitches show.

5. Cut fringe.

6. Add bead or quill strip.

Blanket Leggings

1. Made basically the same as Sioux.

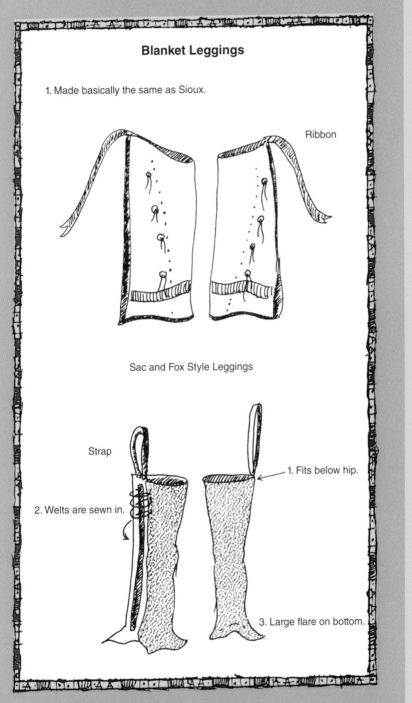

Ribbon

Sac and Fox Style Leggings

Strap

1. Fits below hip.

2. Welts are sewn in.

3. Large flare on bottom.

Breech Clout

This was a must of the times. They were made of soft buckskin or cloth. It varied in length according to the tribe. The Sac or Fox clouts were so short they looked like diapers.

1. Cut out of wool blanket, red or blue trade cloth, or buckskin.

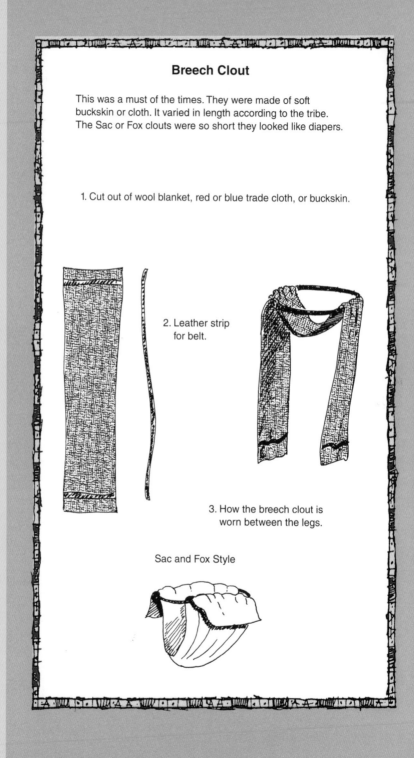

2. Leather strip for belt.

3. How the breech clout is worn between the legs.

Sac and Fox Style

Capote
(Blanket Coat)

The Hudson Bay Company was established in the territories of England to establish a fur trade with the Native Americans. Among one of the prized trade items was the Hudson Bay 4–point trade blanket. When the American Indian obtained one of these blankets, it was then cut and sewn into a hooded coat that could keep the chill off at low winter temperatures.

This coat, used by both Native Americans and mountain men, is a good all-weather warm coat which can stand heavy usage. Typically, it was made from a Hudson Bay Blanket, but any good quality woolen blanket will do. The instructions for making the coat are as follows.

Instructions

1. Enlarge the pattern onto a large piece of paper. Several sheets of newspaper taped together will do. Make sure that the measurements for the back length, A to E, and for the sleeve length, A to C and C to F are accurate. Take the sleeve measurement as shown in the drawing with the arm at the side.

2. Lay out the pattern pieces on the blanket which has been folded in half lengthwise. Adjust the pieces on the strips to obtain the best proportions. After cutting out the body and the hood and tassels, the sleeve pieces may be folded in half to facilitate cutting.

3. With right sides together, using a 5/8″ seam, sew the shoulder seam CD.

4. With right sides together sew the underarm seam DG.

5. Place the sleeve in the armhole with the wrong sides together, the sleeve extending into the body and the fringe sticking out of the armhole. Align the seam lines, CD, sew and cut the fringe.

6. With right sides together, sew the hood seam H I placing the small ends of the tassels in the seam at point I with the tassels on the inside.

7. Fold the hood fringe back to the outside along line BJ and stitch ½″ from the fold and hold it in place. Cut the fringe.

8. To sew the hood to the capote, place the right side of the hood to the wrong side of the capote making sure to match points B. Point A on the body should match point H on the hood at the center back. Stitch, cut the fringe, which will fold back to cover the stitching, and whip stitch the inner seam allowance to the capote.

9. On the outside, cover the armhole and shoulder seams with the grosgrain ribbon.

10. Bind all the raw edges of the front and cuff with ribbon and the front edge of the hood as well. The hem may be finished with ribbon, or a fringe may be cut, whichever is desired.

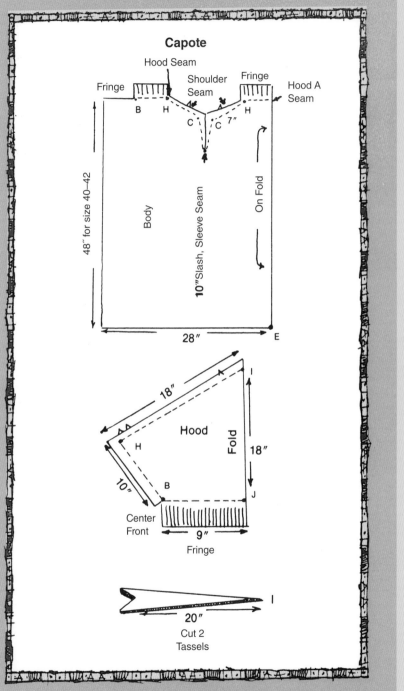

Capote

Hood Seam

Shoulder Seam

Fringe

Fringe

Hood A Seam

B   H

C   C   7"

48" for size 40–42

Body

On Fold

10" Slash, Sleeve Seam

28"

E

83

18"

Hood

Fold

18"

H

B   J

10"

Center Front

9"

Fringe

20"

Cut 2
Tassels

CLOTHING

Capote
(continued)

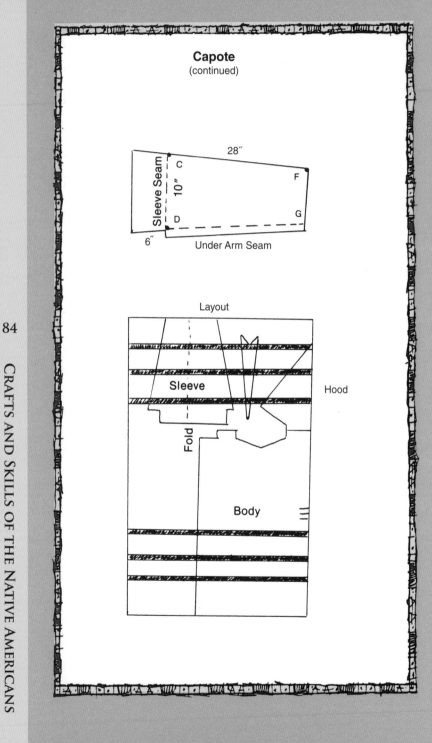

28″

Sleeve Seam

10″

C

F

D

G

6″

Under Arm Seam

Layout

Sleeve

Hood

Fold

Body

Capote

(continued)

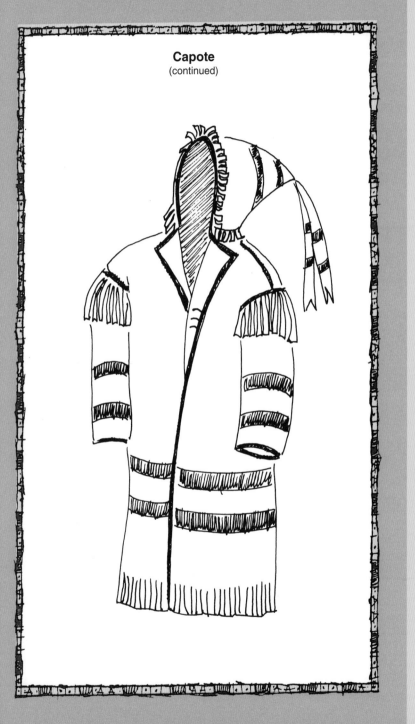

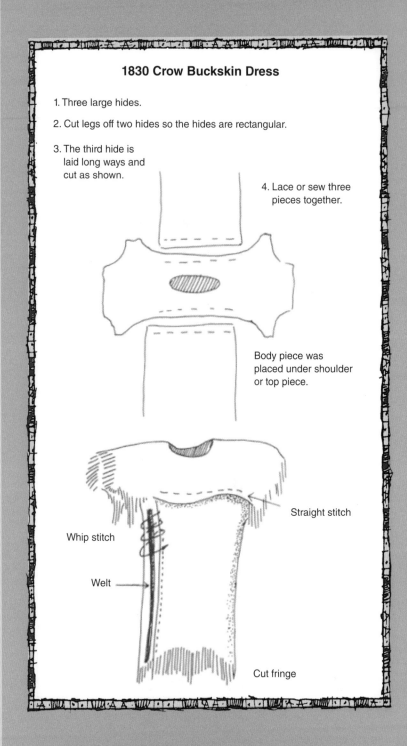

1830 Crow Buckskin Dress

1. Three large hides.

2. Cut legs off two hides so the hides are rectangular.

3. The third hide is laid long ways and cut as shown.

4. Lace or sew three pieces together.

Body piece was placed under shoulder or top piece.

Straight stitch

Whip stitch

Welt

Cut fringe

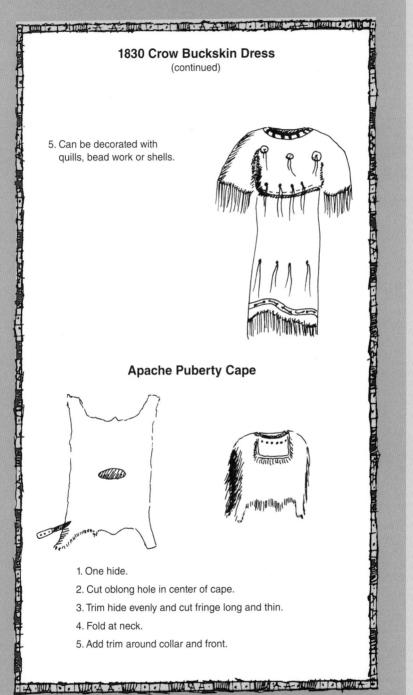

1830 Crow Buckskin Dress
(continued)

5. Can be decorated with
   quills, bead work or shells.

Apache Puberty Cape

1. One hide.

2. Cut oblong hole in center of cape.

3. Trim hide evenly and cut fringe long and thin.

4. Fold at neck.

5. Add trim around collar and front.

CLOTHING

Sioux Cloth Dress

When trade cloth was introduced to the Sioux, they fashioned a very pretty black, red, and white dress that was good for summer use as well as special occasions.

Today, since many mountain man activities are held in the summer, a buckskin dress would be warm, so a decorative cotton dress would be the answer to keeping cool at Rendezvous.

The material is not expensive and can be purchased at most fabric shops.

Cowrie shells can sometimes be purchased at craft stores.

The Sioux Indian Dress is made of cotton or flannel with the colors being red, black and white. It can be trimmed with cowrie shells or elks teeth if you're fortunate enough to have that many. Plastic elks teeth are made, but most people don't like to use plastic. This dress is loose, airy and quite comfortable in the summer.

Instructions

1. Make either with black body and red border or the opposite, in either case, with white ¼″ twill tape trim.

2. Measure elbow to elbow, shoulder to finished length, chest to which you need to add about five inches, and last, the head measurement to determine the neck size.

3. Lay out the body fabric as shown and draw the pattern on with tailor's chalk. This dress is loose; the underarm cut should not be too shallow—midbody below the bust line is about right. It might be a good idea to have the person for whom the dress is intended lie down on the fabric and trace the pattern around her body.

4. Open out the cut-out body fabric and trace onto paper the correct shapes for the sleeve and hem border. Then draw a large oval shape which should be at least as wide as the person's shoulders. Cut this out of paper and check it on the fabric to be

sure that the shape looks good. Then cut these shapes out of the contrasting fabric.

5. Mark the head measurement with tailor's chalk onto the wrong side of the neck border. Do not cut it out yet. Lay the right side of the neck border on the wrong side of the body piece and sew around the marked neck edge. Cut out the neck hole, clip and curve, turn it to the right side, and press. Lay the right side of the arm borders on the wrong side of the body and sew the outside edge. Trim the seam, clip the corners and turn and press.

6. Sew the loose edge of both neck and arm borders. Then add the twill tape trim to both edges of the border, covering the raw edge of the border fabric.

7. Sew the dress side seams, right sides together. Turn and press. Sew the side seams of the hem border. Turn and press.

8. Attach the bottom border in the same manner as the other borders, i.e., sew hem edges, right sides together, then turn, press, sew the raw edge down and add trim.

9. Sew the decorations on by hand, using as few or as many as desired. Sew the bottom edge of the sleeve together in at least three places with the decoration, one on each side.

Sioux Cloth Dress

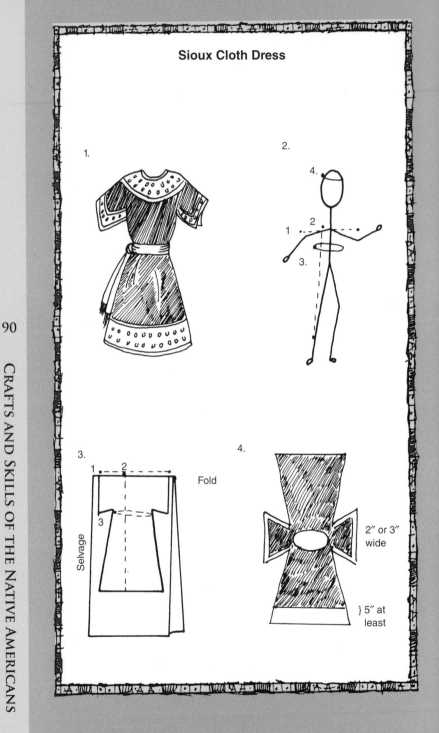

1.

2.

4.

1

2

3.

3.

1   2

Fold

Selvage

3

4.

2" or 3"
wide

} 5" at
least

Sioux Cloth Dress
(continued)

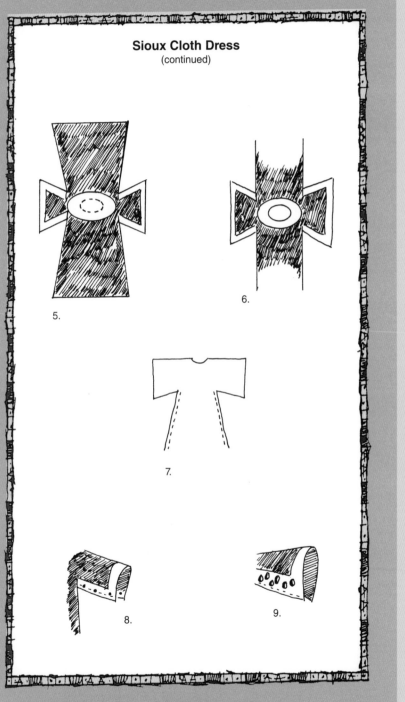

5.

6.

7.

8.

9.

Moccasins

The terrain determined what type of moccasin was worn. Archeological finds have shown that sandals seemed to be the forerunner for American Indian footwear, though.

Determine what kind of terrain you will make your moccasin for and go from there. If you are going to be on rocks and hard ground with cacti around, soft soles are not what you want. On the other hand, if you're going to do some stalking in wooded areas on soft forest floors, a good Seneca or one-piece Plains-style soft-soled moccasin would be just the thing.

One-Piece Plains Moccasin

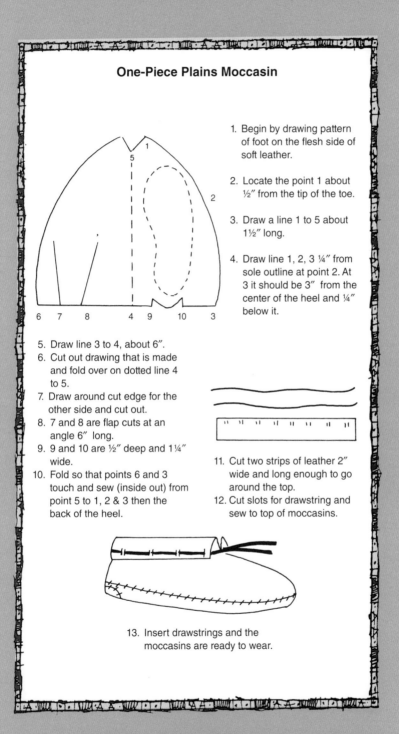

1. Begin by drawing pattern of foot on the flesh side of soft leather.

2. Locate the point 1 about ½″ from the tip of the toe.

3. Draw a line 1 to 5 about 1½″ long.

4. Draw line 1, 2, 3 ¼″ from sole outline at point 2. At 3 it should be 3″ from the center of the heel and ¼″ below it.

5. Draw line 3 to 4, about 6″.
6. Cut out drawing that is made and fold over on dotted line 4 to 5.
7. Draw around cut edge for the other side and cut out.
8. 7 and 8 are flap cuts at an angle 6″ long.
9. 9 and 10 are ½″ deep and 1¼″ wide.
10. Fold so that points 6 and 3 touch and sew (inside out) from point 5 to 1, 2 & 3 then the back of the heel.

11. Cut two strips of leather 2″ wide and long enough to go around the top.
12. Cut slots for drawstring and sew to top of moccasins.

13. Insert drawstrings and the moccasins are ready to wear.

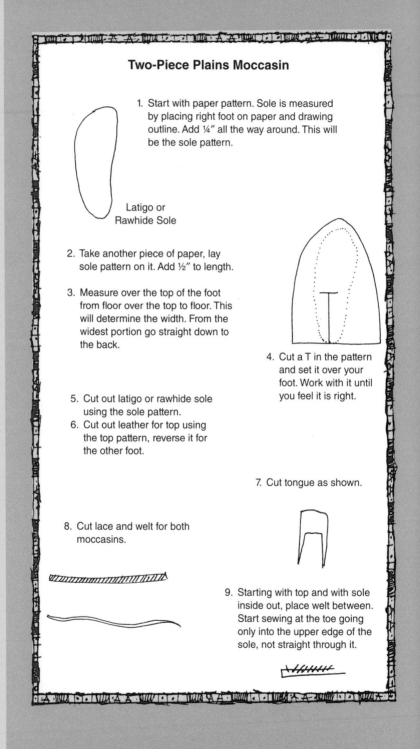

Two-Piece Plains Moccasin

1. Start with paper pattern. Sole is measured by placing right foot on paper and drawing outline. Add ¼″ all the way around. This will be the sole pattern.

Latigo or
Rawhide Sole

2. Take another piece of paper, lay sole pattern on it. Add ½″ to length.

3. Measure over the top of the foot from floor over the top to floor. This will determine the width. From the widest portion go straight down to the back.

4. Cut a T in the pattern and set it over your foot. Work with it until you feel it is right.

5. Cut out latigo or rawhide sole using the sole pattern.
6. Cut out leather for top using the top pattern, reverse it for the other foot.

7. Cut tongue as shown.

8. Cut lace and welt for both moccasins.

9. Starting with top and with sole inside out, place welt between. Start sewing at the toe going only into the upper edge of the sole, not straight through it.

Two-Piece Plains Moccasin
(continued)

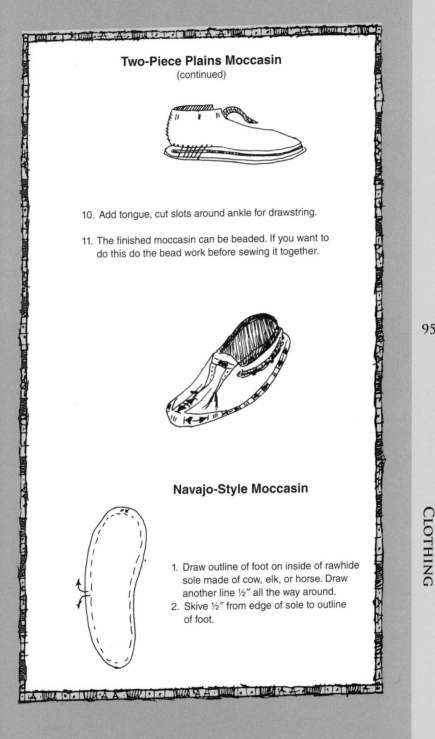

10. Add tongue, cut slots around ankle for drawstring.

11. The finished moccasin can be beaded. If you want to do this do the bead work before sewing it together.

Navajo-Style Moccasin

1. Draw outline of foot on inside of rawhide sole made of cow, elk, or horse. Draw another line ½" all the way around.
2. Skive ½" from edge of sole to outline of foot.

Navajo-Style Moccasin
(continued)

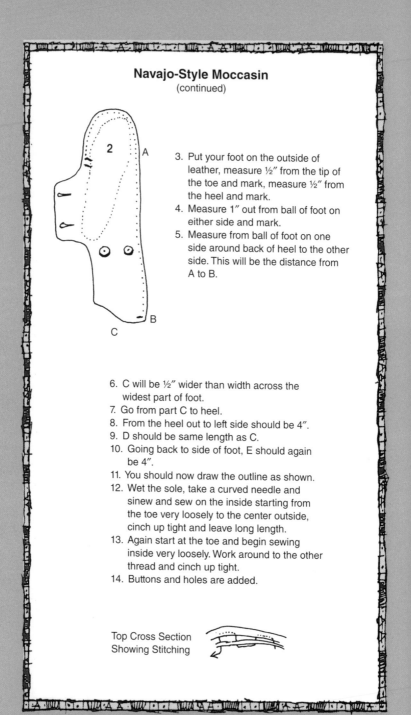

3. Put your foot on the outside of leather, measure ½″ from the tip of the toe and mark, measure ½″ from the heel and mark.
4. Measure 1″ out from ball of foot on either side and mark.
5. Measure from ball of foot on one side around back of heel to the other side. This will be the distance from A to B.

6. C will be ½″ wider than width across the widest part of foot.
7. Go from part C to heel.
8. From the heel out to left side should be 4″.
9. D should be same length as C.
10. Going back to side of foot, E should again be 4″.
11. You should now draw the outline as shown.
12. Wet the sole, take a curved needle and sinew and sew on the inside starting from the toe very loosely to the center outside, cinch up tight and leave long length.
13. Again start at the toe and begin sewing inside very loosely. Work around to the other thread and cinch up tight.
14. Buttons and holes are added.

Top Cross Section
Showing Stitching

Navajo-Style Moccasin
(continued)

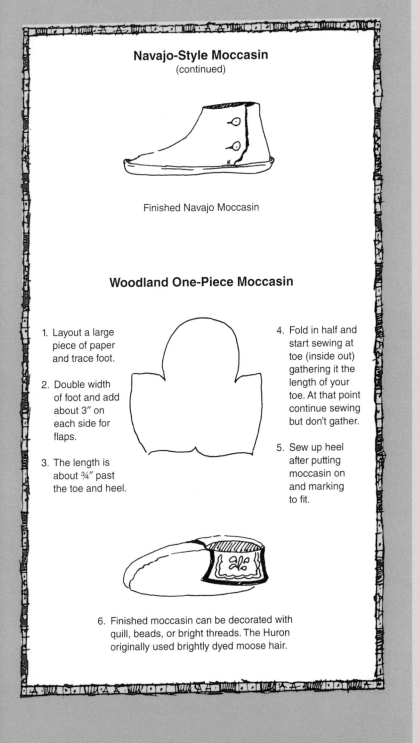

Finished Navajo Moccasin

Woodland One-Piece Moccasin

1. Layout a large piece of paper and trace foot.

2. Double width of foot and add about 3″ on each side for flaps.

3. The length is about ¾″ past the toe and heel.

4. Fold in half and start sewing at toe (inside out) gathering it the length of your toe. At that point continue sewing but don't gather.

5. Sew up heel after putting moccasin on and marking to fit.

6. Finished moccasin can be decorated with quill, beads, or bright threads. The Huron originally used brightly dyed moose hair.

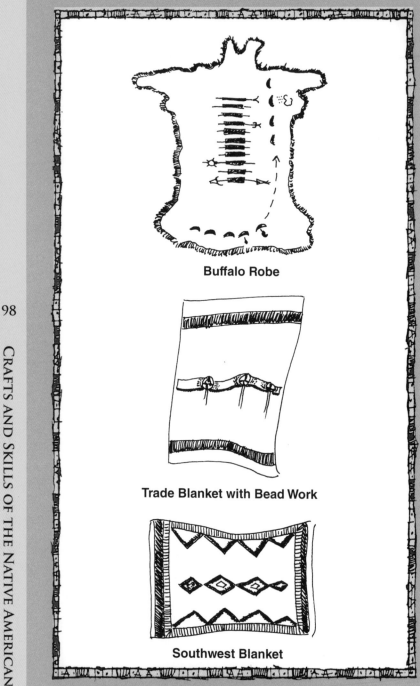

Buffalo Robe

Trade Blanket with Bead Work

Southwest Blanket

CRAFTS AND SKILLS OF THE NATIVE AMERICANS

Headdresses

Womens' Pomo and
Paiute Head Basket

Osage fur hat, open on top
with bead work around top
edge.

Iroquois, Wea, or Delaware
wore cloth turbans.

Crow War Bonnet

1. Make cap of hide to fit
   head slots for thong.

2. Glue and tie
   Marabou (fluff).

3. Glue leather loop
   to base.

4. Add flannel binding
   around base leaving
   loop free.

5. Wrap and tie binding
   with sinew.

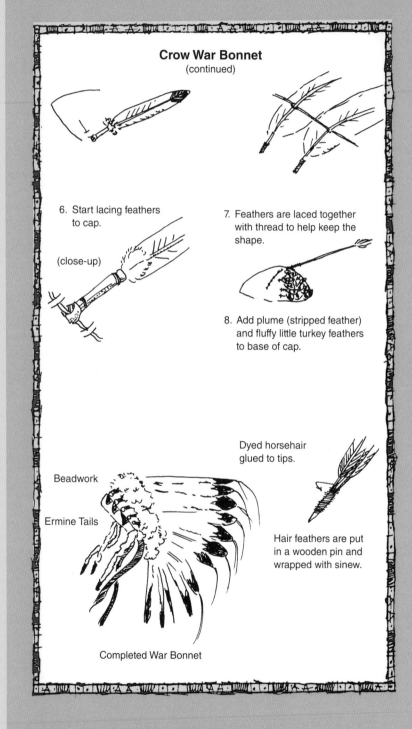

Crow War Bonnet
(continued)

6. Start lacing feathers to cap.

(close-up)

7. Feathers are laced together with thread to help keep the shape.

8. Add plume (stripped feather) and fluffy little turkey feathers to base of cap.

Dyed horsehair glued to tips.

Beadwork

Ermine Tails

Hair feathers are put in a wooden pin and wrapped with sinew.

Completed War Bonnet

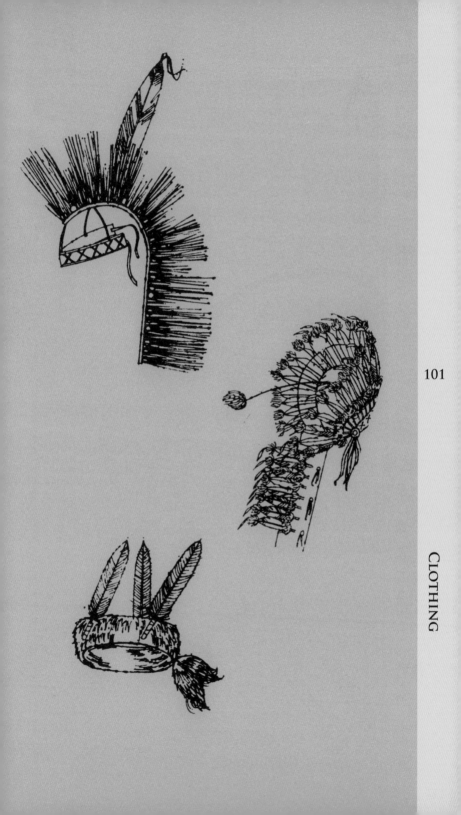

As in the other chapters, nature was the provider. Cooking and eating ware consisted of wooden and clay bowls, horn spoons, basket grain-holders, paunch boiling containers, bark pails, and grinding stones to name a few.

The cooking fire was started with friction sticks or flint and steel.

Most of these items are easily made yet are very important to the stomach.

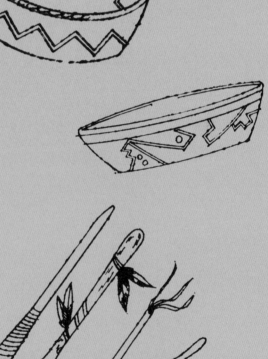

Chapter 7

Cooking and Eating Utensils

Hide or Paunch Cooking

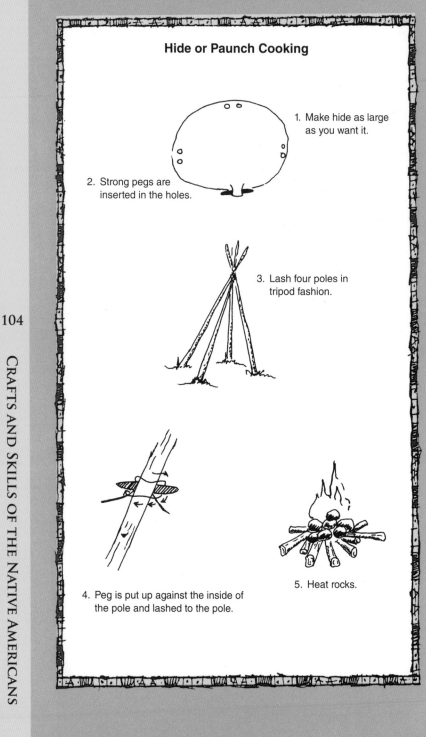

1. Make hide as large as you want it.

2. Strong pegs are inserted in the holes.

3. Lash four poles in tripod fashion.

4. Peg is put up against the inside of the pole and lashed to the pole.

5. Heat rocks.

Hide or Paunch Cooking
(continued)

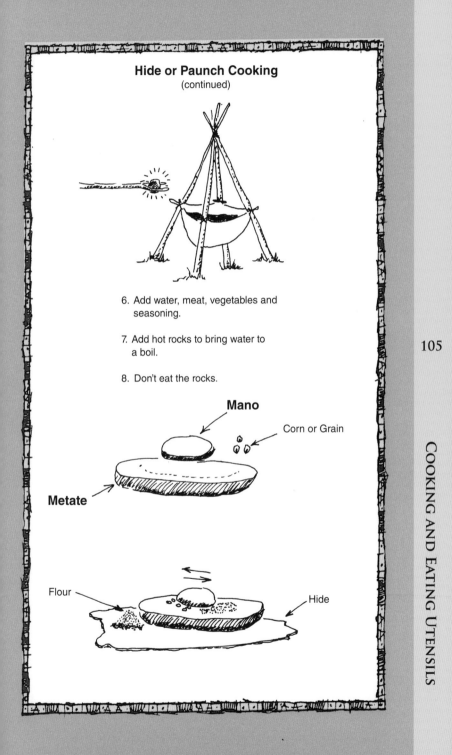

6. Add water, meat, vegetables and seasoning.

7. Add hot rocks to bring water to a boil.

8. Don't eat the rocks.

Mano

Corn or Grain

Metate

Flour

Hide

Wooden Bowl

1. Section of dried log marked, then carved on the outside.

2. Inside can be carved out with an Abnaki (crooked knife) by pulling around the inside.

Southwest Cooking Pot

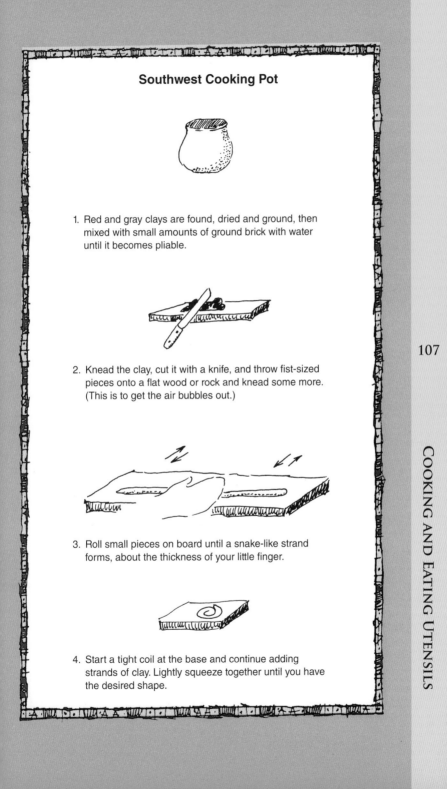

1. Red and gray clays are found, dried and ground, then mixed with small amounts of ground brick with water until it becomes pliable.

2. Knead the clay, cut it with a knife, and throw fist-sized pieces onto a flat wood or rock and knead some more. (This is to get the air bubbles out.)

3. Roll small pieces on board until a snake-like strand forms, about the thickness of your little finger.

4. Start a tight coil at the base and continue adding strands of clay. Lightly squeeze together until you have the desired shape.

Southwest Cooking Pot
(continued)

5. Once you have your clay shaped, put one hand inside, using a small, flat scraper in the other hand and smooth the outside then the inside.

6. Put in a cool, dry place. Dry slowly to prevent cracking.

7. When dry, take the shape and apply slip (watered-down clay) and rub it on the surface. If a high sheen is desired, it must be rubbed with a smooth flint to polish.

New Pot

Pot Shards

Cow Pies

8. Cow pies or sheep dung are used for firing. Place on a good foot of dried manure about 3′ × 3′ wide. Take broken pottery and set on top, placing the new pot in the center.

Southwest Cooking Pot
(continued)

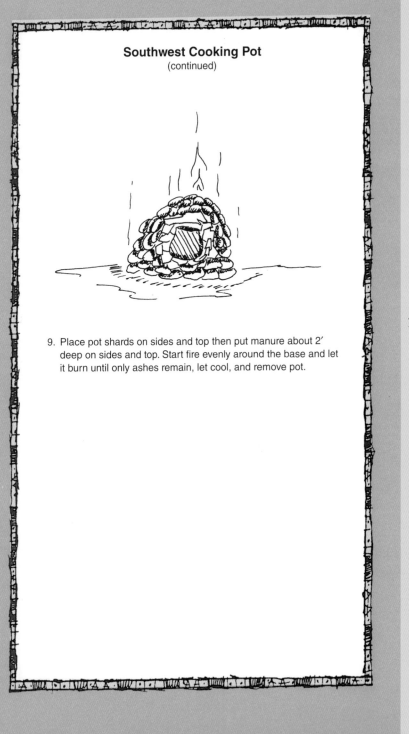

9. Place pot shards on sides and top then put manure about 2′
   deep on sides and top. Start fire evenly around the base and let
   it burn until only ashes remain, let cool, and remove pot.

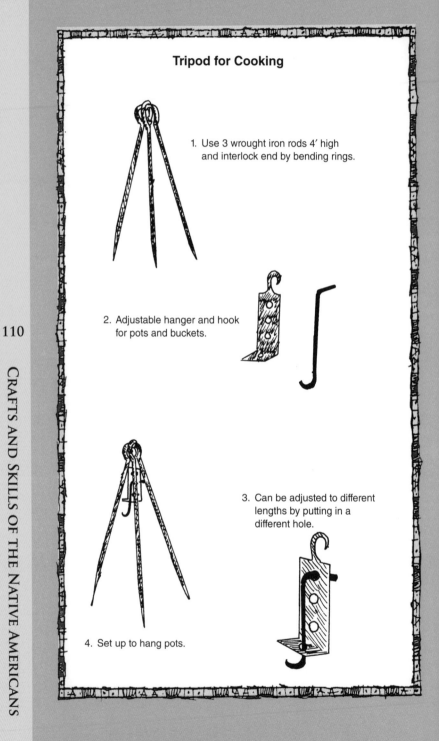

Tripod for Cooking

1. Use 3 wrought iron rods 4' high and interlock end by bending rings.

2. Adjustable hanger and hook for pots and buckets.

3. Can be adjusted to different lengths by putting in a different hole.

4. Set up to hang pots.

CRAFTS AND SKILLS OF THE NATIVE AMERICANS

Horn Spoon

1. Horn spoons made from buffalo, big horn sheep or elk were common among many of the tribes. Good cow horn will work.

2. Clean inside of horn out, then scrape and file the surface.

3. Sand and rub if you want it smoother.

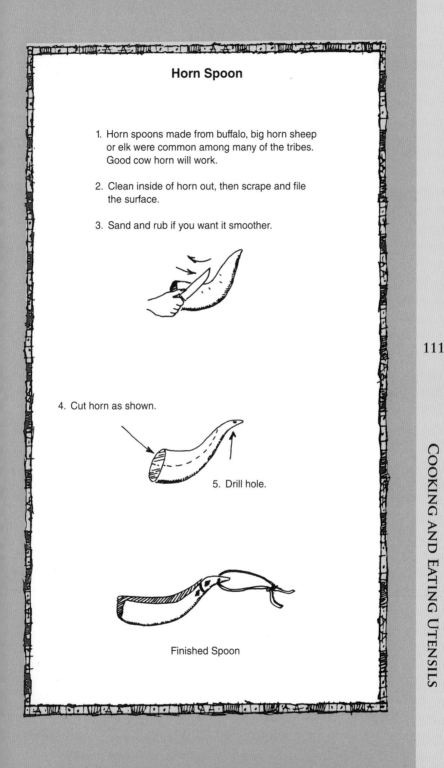

4. Cut horn as shown.

5. Drill hole.

Finished Spoon

No food, no life! The life of the Native American was centered around the need to find nourishment. Due to nature's way of doing things, there were times of famine as well as times of plenty. On the plains, the Native American moved with the buffalo herds. The Pueblos depended on rain for crops and when there were droughts, starvation wiped out whole communities. Digger Indians ate roots and insects, while the Eskimo ate seal and caribou. Those who lived along rivers sustained life with fish as their main diet.

Much of the food from that era can still be found today with a few exceptions. Remember that any wild foods must be obtained legally, and be sure you know for certain what plant you are gathering. It only takes one bite of "death camas" to do you in.

CHAPTER 8
FOODS

List of Common Native American Foods

Acorn

Antelope

Beans

Bear

Beaver

Birds

Buffalo

Caribou

Chokecherries

Corn

Crabapple

Currants

Deer

Eggs

Elk

Fish

Hickory nut oil

Locust tree blossoms

Maple sugar

Mescal

Mountain sheep

Pine nuts

Prickly pear cactus fruit

Pumpkin

Rabbit

Squash

Sumac berries

Sweet potato

Turnips

Watermelon

Wild berries

Wild onions

Wild rice

Yucca—central stem of narrow leaf

Yucca fruit

Drinks

Wintergreen—leaves

Spruce leaves

Red raspberry—twigs

Chokecherry—twigs

Wild cherry—twigs

Seasonings

Mountain mint—flowers and buds, for meat or broth

Wild ginger—root put in with cooking meat (also good for digestion)

Corn silk—dried by the fire and put in a broth

Vegetables

Jerusalem artichoke—root eaten like a radish

Arrowhead—root, strung and dried and later boiled

White pine moss—boiled and put in a fish or meat broth

Common milkweed—flower, cut up and stewed

Bullrush—bulb at the end of the root, sweet in summer, eaten raw

Aspen syrup—between the bark and the wood

Food Preparation

Wild Rice—Menominee (Algonkian), Chippewas

Wild rice was harvested in the Lake Superior and Lake Michigan regions but it was not actually a rice. Stalks were bent over the boat and beaten with a paddle, then the stalk was released. Next it was dried in the sun then beaten again to remove the hull. It was placed in a bark tray or blanket and winnowed with the wind. After that the wild rice was washed three or four times. Prepared by boiling in two parts water to one part rice with one or two spoonsful of maple sugar added, or the rice was cooked in a stew.

Fish—*All tribes near waters containing fish (except Blackfoot, Crow and Comanche)*

Catch fish either by net, spear, trap, or line, then clean. For preservation, fish were smoked or dried over low heat and placed on green sticks high enough above the fire so that the sticks didn't burn. If fish were to be eaten fresh they were either put in the ashes to roast, or encased in clay and broiled in the coals, or placed on pronged sticks to roast over a fire.

Corn—*All farming tribes*

To roast the corn, put it—husk and all—into the raked-out fire pit (after a hot fire) then put cold ashes over it with a layer of hot coals on top of this. Roast for about 10 to 15 minutes. Remove corn from pit, clean off the husk, and eat.

To parch the corn, strip the kernels from the cob and place them in a pan filled with salt and mix it until the corn is covered. Set above the fire. It is done when the corn is brown and swollen. When ready to use, pound into a fine meal which can then be mixed with dried berries.

Cattail—*Most tribes*

The root was washed and eaten raw, or boiled, or dried and pounded into a flour for bread.

Squash—*Farming tribes*

Put the whole squash in hot ashes and bake it. You can also eat the seeds—shell and all.

Chokecherries—*Western tribes*

After it was picked and the seeds taken out (poisonous), it was sun dried for storage, then eaten as dried fruit or pounded to mix with corn flour or pemmican.

Prickly Pear Cactus Fruit—*Southwestern tribes*

Harvest the buds prior to flowering and cut the outer skin off. This was eaten as is or mixed in with stews.

Jerky—*All tribes*

There are many ways to fix jerky, but the original way was very simple. Native Americans used the meat of buffalo, deer, elk, or goat. The meat is cut into thin strips about 2 inches wide and 6 inches long then laid over sticks or on flat rocks in the hot sun or near a fire to dry until it becomes leathery. Some tribes used salt on it and if you want a little more flavor you can add pepper. (Pepper is not a common American Indian spice, of course.) When jerky is dry, store it in a cool place.

Pemmican—*Most tribes*

This is a good winter survival food that can really be a lifesaver. The food was prepared for long storage and was very nutritional. To make pemmican, grind jerky into a powder. (The amount depends on how much you are making.) Take dried berries (cherry, raisins, currants, etc.) and grind jerky and berries together. The American Indians did this with a stone maul or mano and metate. Take the kidney or loin fat from beef (originally made from buffalo), melt over a fire until it is clear, then mix this with the berries and meat powder until it sticks together. Shape into balls the size of fists or smaller. Lay out flat and cut into pieces when it is cooled. Store in a cool place. It is possible to save this for a year or two but the taste of stored pemmican might not suit you. Pemmican was originally stored in rawhide bags. (Do not use deer or elk fat.)

Eggs—*Coastal and lakeshore Indians*

Duck, bird, turtle, and alligator eggs were harvested in marshy areas. Today you must check on laws concerning the collection of wild birds' eggs. Most are not legal to gather. Boiled eggs were eaten by the Native American as we eat them today. The eggs were placed in a paunch of boiling water, or with the stew, and were cooked for about five minutes, Removed, they were shelled, and eaten. Another method used was to crack the raw egg into the stew, or soup, and cook it in the broth.

Waterfowl—*Palutes and lake tribes*

Waterfowl must be taken only in season and only with legal methods. Nets and traps were originally used. When a waterfowl is killed, cut the head off the bird immediately to bleed it. This will rid the meat of the muddy taste, to some degree. Clean it out and skin it rather than plucking the feathers. Skewer the bird through the middle with a green stick and prop it over a fire high enough for it to cook slowly, turning it often.

Both the nomadic and farmer American Indians had, at one time, quite a lot of food provided by mother nature and they used it wisely. When the white man arrived, the Indians' food sources were terminated to a great degree. Today, some of those food sources are still there, but laws, and good common sense, will dictate the use of these sources.

Wild Plants for Medicine

Headache—Dogbane: root, dried and pulverized. Four small pea-sized pieces ground and snuffed up the nostrils.

Headache—Yarrow: leaves, decoction, sprinkled on hot stones and fumes inhaled.

Cold—Calamus: root, pulverized, snuffed up nostrils.

Cold and cough—Burdock: leaves, a handful steeped in a cup of boiling water taken after a coughing spell for a hard, dry cough.

Sore throat—Chokecherry: inner bark decoction gargled.

Indigestion—Wild Ginger: root, sliced and cooked with food.

Indigestion—Arrowhead: root, steep in water then drink.

Colic—Hedgenettle: leaves, steep in hot water then drink for sudden hard colic.

Cuts—Aspen Bark: spit on the cut and draw the edges together, chew the bark and apply this as a poultice.

Poisonous bites—Plantain: fresh leaves and root, chopped and applied to the bite.

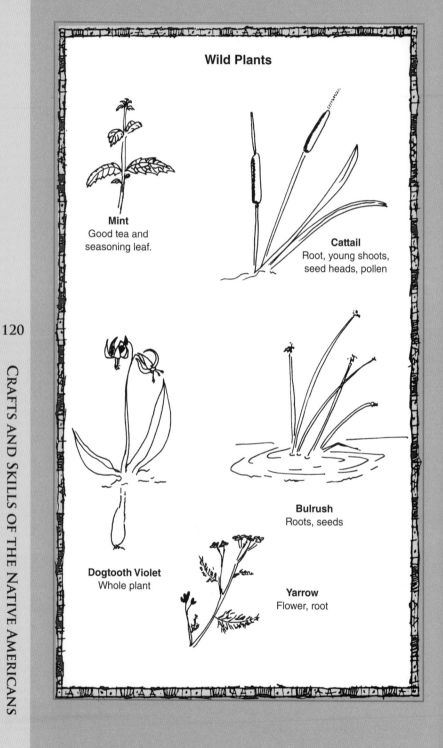

Wild Plants

Mint
Good tea and
seasoning leaf.

Cattail
Root, young shoots,
seed heads, pollen

Dogtooth Violet
Whole plant

Bulrush
Roots, seeds

Yarrow
Flower, root

Wild Plants
(continued)

Plantain
Leaf

Indian Potato
Root

Burdock
Root, burr, leaf

Chokecherry
Fruit

Wild Ginger
Root

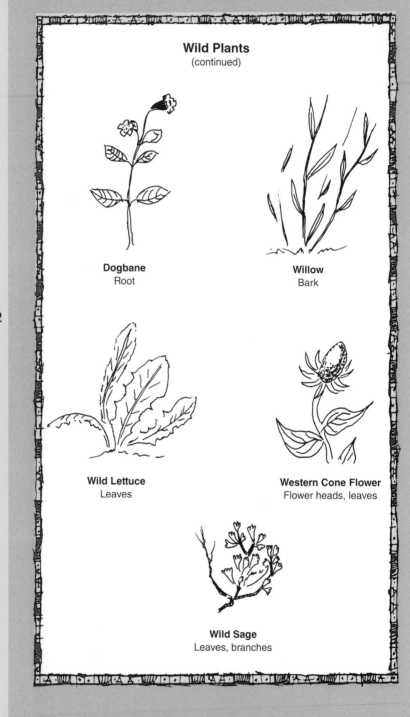

Wild Plants
(continued)

Dogbane
Root

Willow
Bark

Wild Lettuce
Leaves

Western Cone Flower
Flower heads, leaves

Wild Sage
Leaves, branches

Wild Plants
(continued)

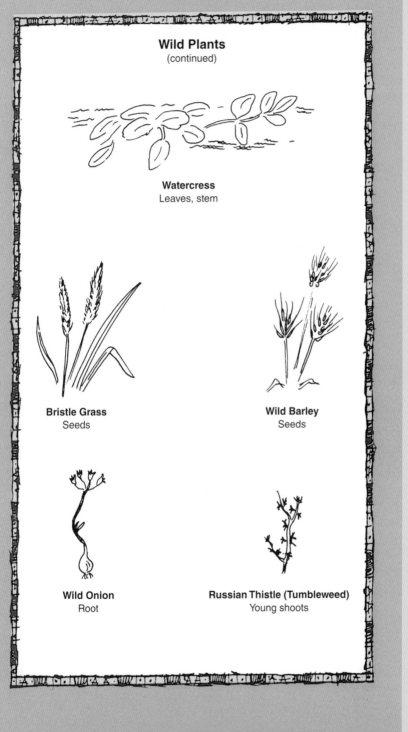

Watercress
Leaves, stem

Bristle Grass
Seeds

Wild Barley
Seeds

Wild Onion
Root

Russian Thistle (Tumbleweed)
Young shoots

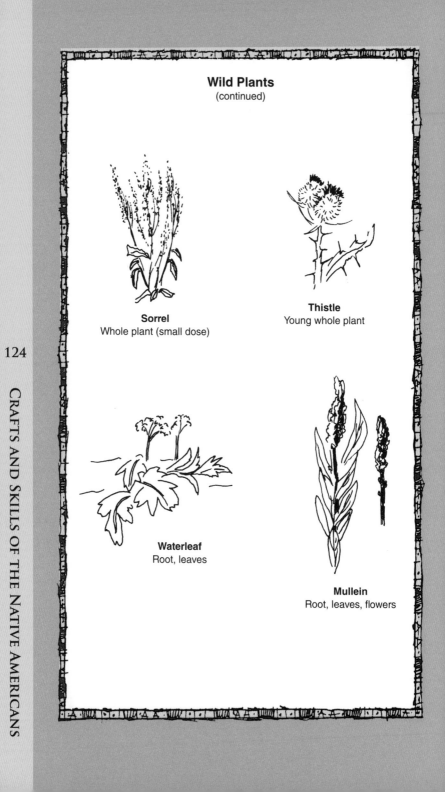

Wild Plants
(continued)

Sorrel
Whole plant (small dose)

Thistle
Young whole plant

Waterleaf
Root, leaves

Mullein
Root, leaves, flowers

124

Wild Plants
(continued)

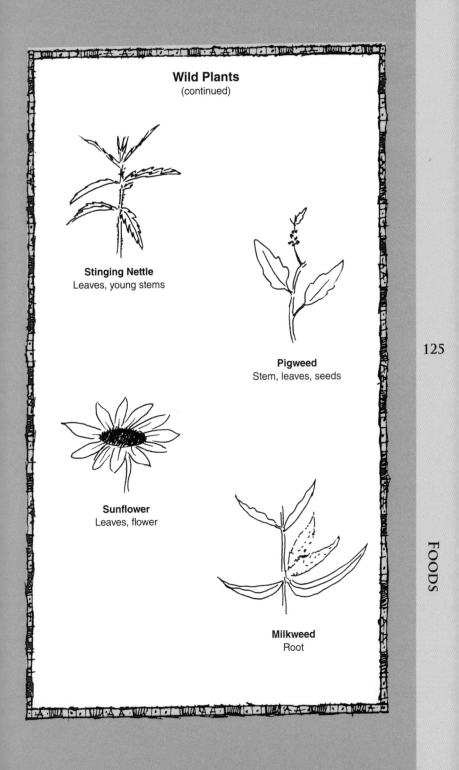

Stinging Nettle
Leaves, young stems

Pigweed
Stem, leaves, seeds

Sunflower
Leaves, flower

Milkweed
Root

Man, dog, horse, and boat constituted the main modes of transportation for the Native Americans. All four ways to travel are still available today. Many experts claim that the horse was introduced by the Spanish, but ruins that predate the Spanish show carvings of horses and toys have been found in the form of a horse.

Horse and dog and canoe lightened the load and helped make hunting and moving about easier for Native Americans. Several kinds of boats, i.e., canoe, kayak, and dugout, were used extensively in their respective regions for obtaining food as well as for travel. The basic design of the birch bark canoe will give you an idea of how much skill was involved in their construction. Knowing how canoes, saddles, and travoises were made and used might help you build your own.

Horse

Dog

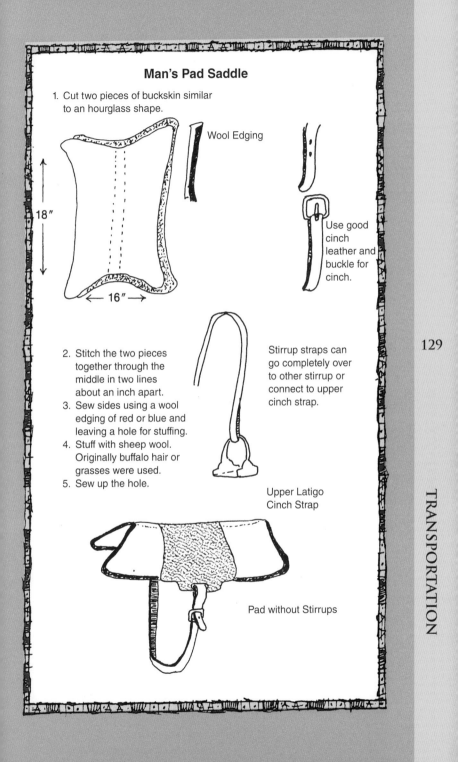

Man's Pad Saddle

1. Cut two pieces of buckskin similar to an hourglass shape.

Wool Edging

18″
16″

Use good cinch leather and buckle for cinch.

2. Stitch the two pieces together through the middle in two lines about an inch apart.
3. Sew sides using a wool edging of red or blue and leaving a hole for stuffing.
4. Stuff with sheep wool. Originally buffalo hair or grasses were used.
5. Sew up the hole.

Stirrup straps can go completely over to other stirrup or connect to upper cinch strap.

Upper Latigo Cinch Strap

Pad without Stirrups

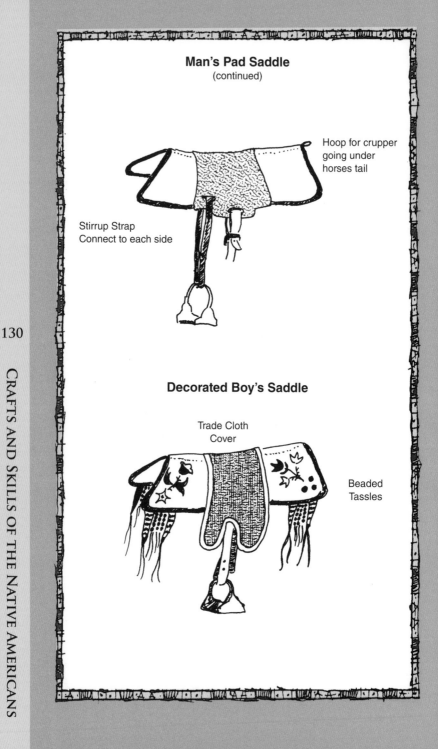

Man's Pad Saddle
(continued)

Hoop for crupper going under horses tail

Stirrup Strap
Connect to each side

Decorated Boy's Saddle

Trade Cloth Cover

Beaded Tassles

Stirrups

1. Cottonwood or poplar wood is used.

2. Carve out parts and tack together.

5½″ × 3½

10″

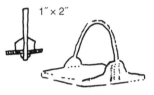

1″ × 2″

3. Cut two pieces of wet rawhide to go on top and on bottom and sew together.

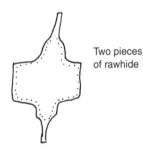

Two pieces
of rawhide

4. Cut two sections of wet rawhide for inner portion of sideboards.

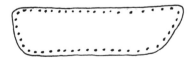

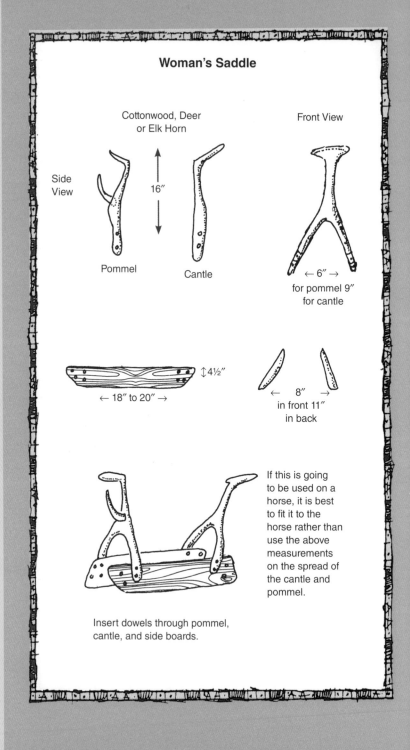

Woman's Saddle

Cottonwood, Deer
or Elk Horn

Front View

Side
View

16″

Pommel

Cantle

← 6″ →
for pommel 9″
for cantle

↕ 4½″

← 18″ to 20″ →

← 8″ →
in front 11″
in back

If this is going
to be used on a
horse, it is best
to fit it to the
horse rather than
use the above
measurements
on the spread of
the cantle and
pommel.

Insert dowels through pommel,
cantle, and side boards.

Woman's Saddle
(continued)

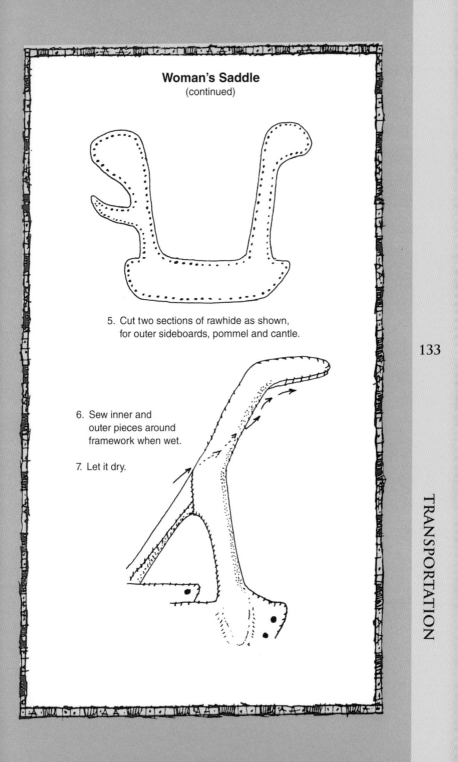

5. Cut two sections of rawhide as shown, for outer sideboards, pommel and cantle.

6. Sew inner and outer pieces around framework when wet.

7. Let it dry.

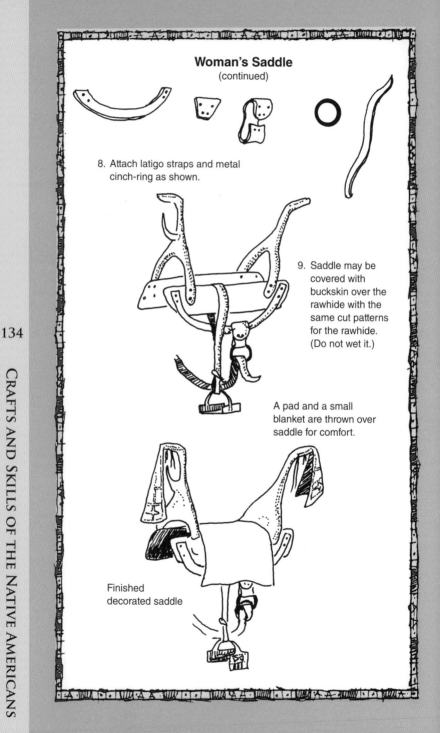

Woman's Saddle
(continued)

8. Attach latigo straps and metal cinch-ring as shown.

9. Saddle may be covered with buckskin over the rawhide with the same cut patterns for the rawhide. (Do not wet it.)

A pad and a small blanket are thrown over saddle for comfort.

Finished decorated saddle

Travois

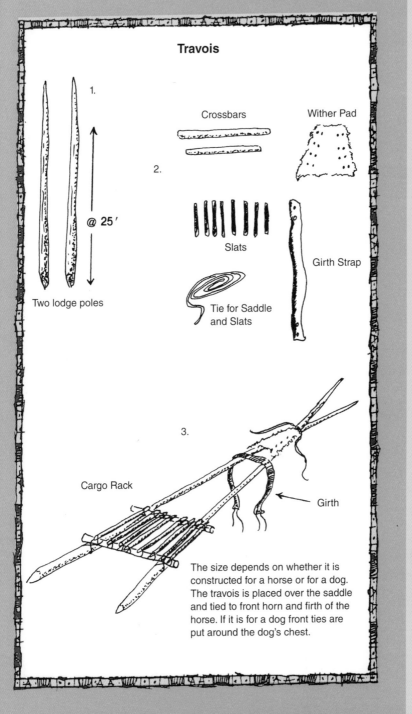

1.

@ 25'

Two lodge poles

2.

Crossbars

Wither Pad

Slats

Girth Strap

Tie for Saddle and Slats

3.

Cargo Rack

Girth

The size depends on whether it is constructed for a horse or for a dog. The travois is placed over the saddle and tied to front horn and firth of the horse. If it is for a dog front ties are put around the dog's chest.

TRANSPORTATION

Birch Bark Canoe
(Ojibwa)

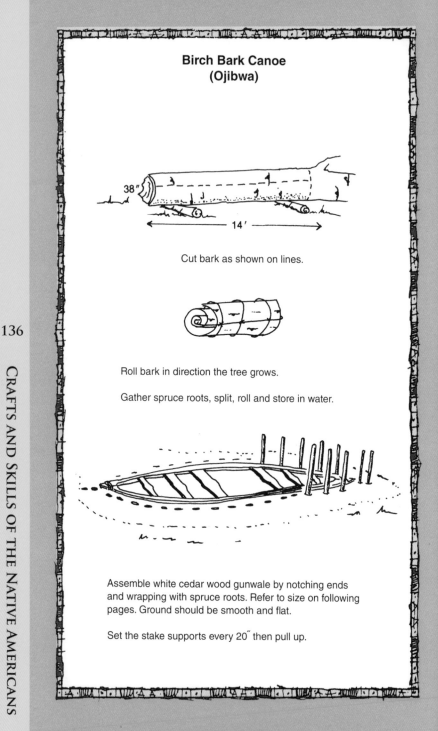

Cut bark as shown on lines.

Roll bark in direction the tree grows.

Gather spruce roots, split, roll and store in water.

Assemble white cedar wood gunwale by notching ends and wrapping with spruce roots. Refer to size on following pages. Ground should be smooth and flat.

Set the stake supports every 20″ then pull up.

Birch Bark Canoe
(continued)

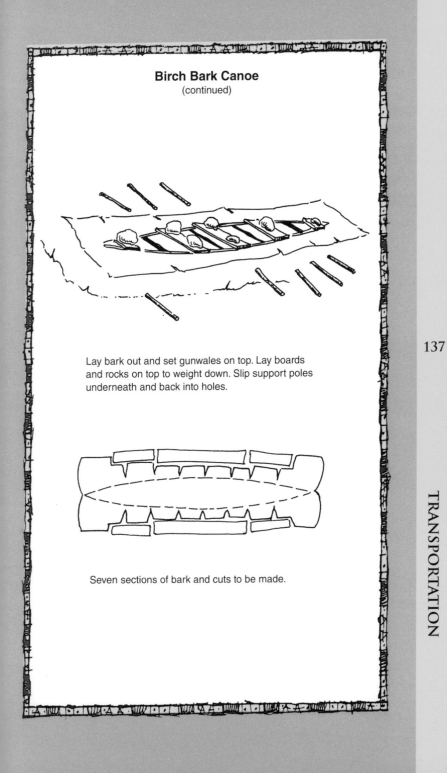

Lay bark out and set gunwales on top. Lay boards and rocks on top to weight down. Slip support poles underneath and back into holes.

Seven sections of bark and cuts to be made.

Birch Bark Canoe
(continued)

Long cedar sticks are put on inside and outside of walls then clamped together with ties.

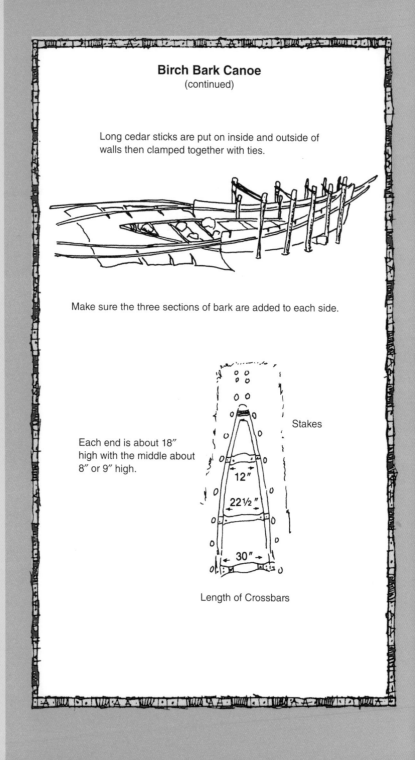

Make sure the three sections of bark are added to each side.

Stakes

Each end is about 18″ high with the middle about 8″ or 9″ high.

12″

22½″

30″

Length of Crossbars

Birch Bark Canoe
(continued)

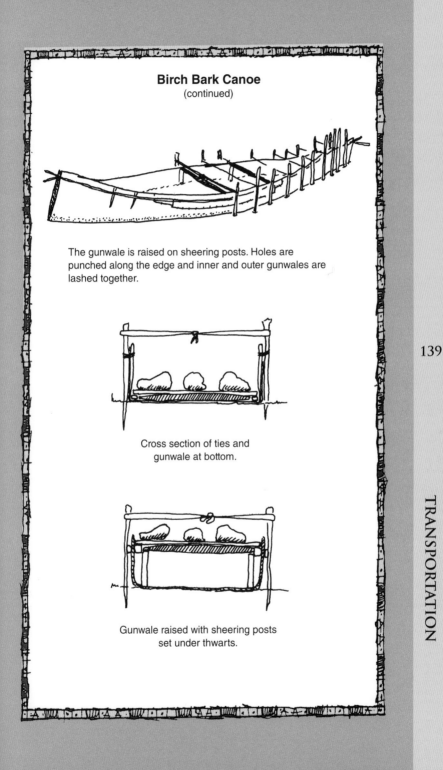

The gunwale is raised on sheering posts. Holes are punched along the edge and inner and outer gunwales are lashed together.

Cross section of ties and
gunwale at bottom.

Gunwale raised with sheering posts
set under thwarts.

Birch Bark Canoe
(continued)

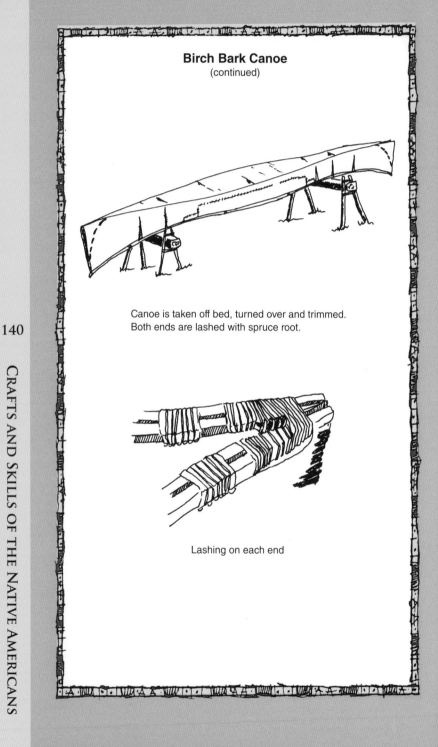

Canoe is taken off bed, turned over and trimmed.
Both ends are lashed with spruce root.

Lashing on each end

140

CRAFTS AND SKILLS OF THE NATIVE AMERICANS

Birch Bark Canoe
(continued)

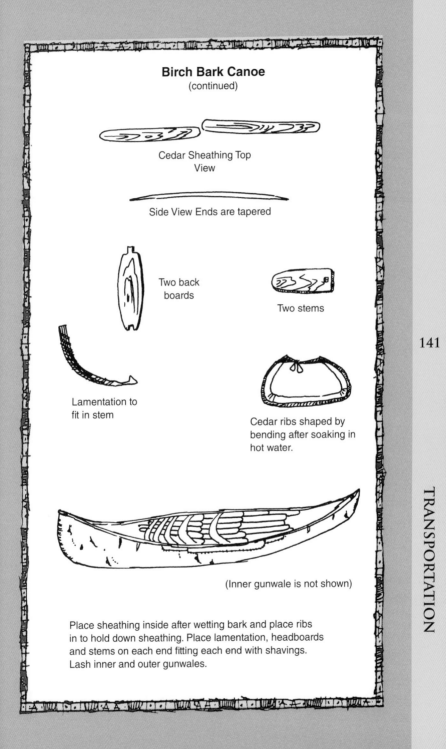

Cedar Sheathing Top
View

Side View Ends are tapered

Two back
boards

Two stems

Lamentation to
fit in stem

Cedar ribs shaped by
bending after soaking in
hot water.

(Inner gunwale is not shown)

Place sheathing inside after wetting bark and place ribs
in to hold down sheathing. Place lamentation, headboards
and stems on each end fitting each end with shavings.
Lash inner and outer gunwales.

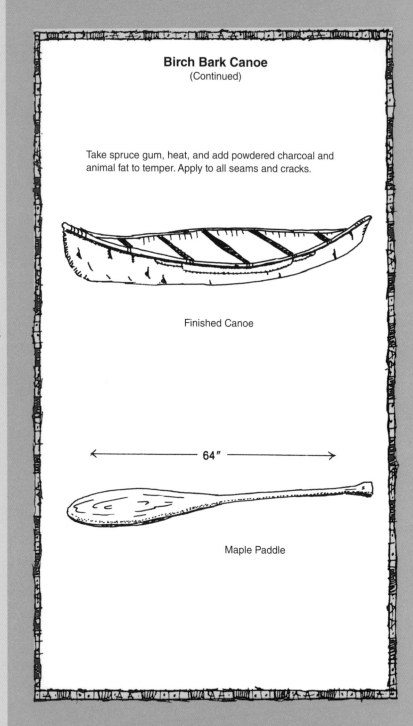

Birch Bark Canoe
(Continued)

Take spruce gum, heat, and add powdered charcoal and animal fat to temper. Apply to all seams and cracks.

Finished Canoe

←——————— 64″ ———————→

Maple Paddle

CRAFTS AND SKILLS OF THE NATIVE AMERICANS

Bullboat

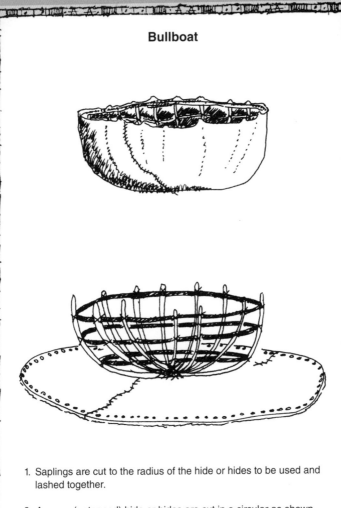

1. Saplings are cut to the radius of the hide or hides to be used and lashed together.

2. A green (untanned) hide or hides are cut in a circular as shown. Sew hides together if one isn't large enough. Buffalo was used but cow hide will work.

3. Burn or punch holes around edge.

4. Pull hide up around top and lace it to the top rail.

5. Let it dry and it's ready to go.

O ne thing is for certain: No Native Americans walked around all day with their hands in their pockets—clothing of their time had none. Still, it was necessary for them to carry certain personal belongings at all times and that meant some type of container. Pouches were made to hold pipes, fire-starting gear, food, knives, arrows, etc. Today we aren't much different; we have purses, wallets, knife and rifle scabbards. We also use suitcases and baby carriers as well as portable chairs. Interesting to note is that these items were all in use before "white man" came. They just had slightly different names, and containers Indians used were usually much more ornate than is today's sleek look. Some of these items will be the easiest of all the grafts in this book to make, but they are some of the most beautiful after they are decorated.

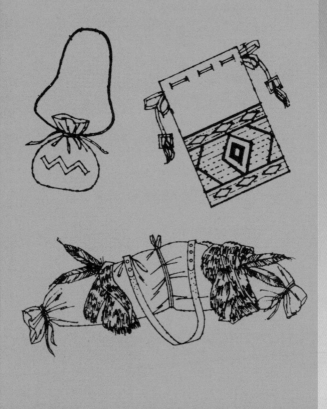

Chapter 10

Pouches, Scabbards, and Assorted Gear

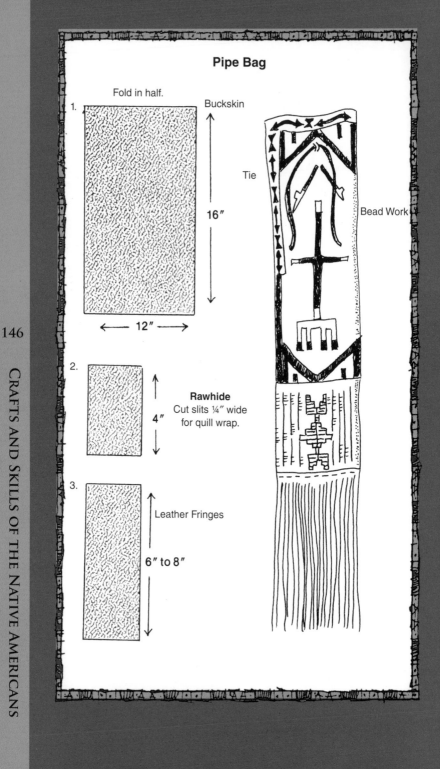

Pipe Bag

Fold in half.

1. Buckskin

Tie

Bead Work

16″

12″

2. Rawhide
Cut slits ¼″ wide
for quill wrap.

4″

3. Leather Fringes

6″ to 8″

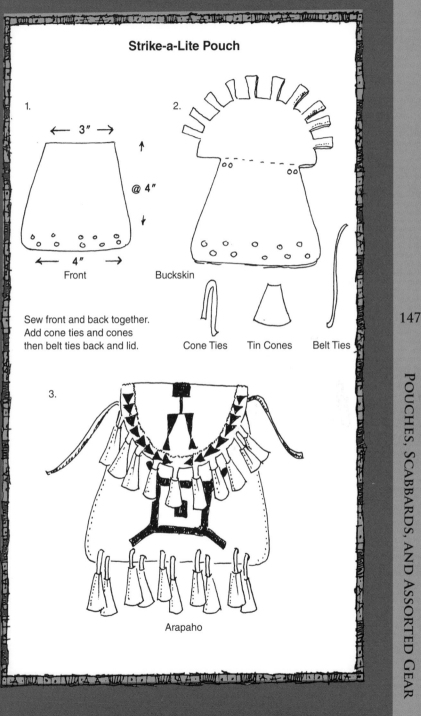

Strike-a-Lite Pouch

1.

← 3″ →

@ 4″

← 4″ →

Front

2.

Buckskin

Sew front and back together.
Add cone ties and cones
then belt ties back and lid.

Cone Ties   Tin Cones   Belt Ties

3.

Arapaho

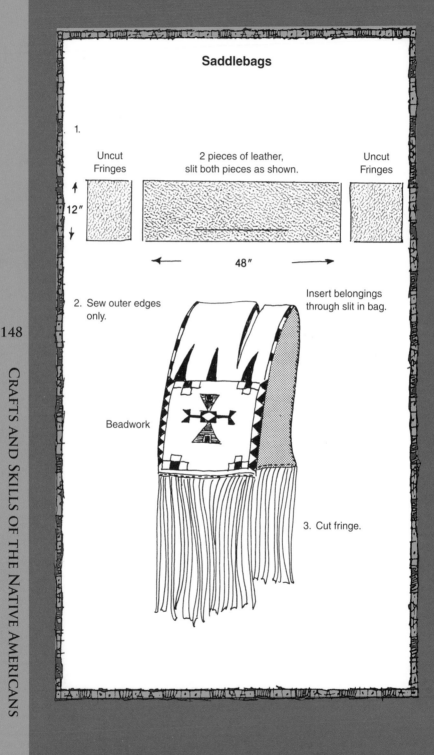

Saddlebags

1.

Uncut Fringes

2 pieces of leather, slit both pieces as shown.

Uncut Fringes

12″

← 48″ →

2. Sew outer edges only.

Insert belongings through slit in bag.

Beadwork

3. Cut fringe.

Knife Scabbard

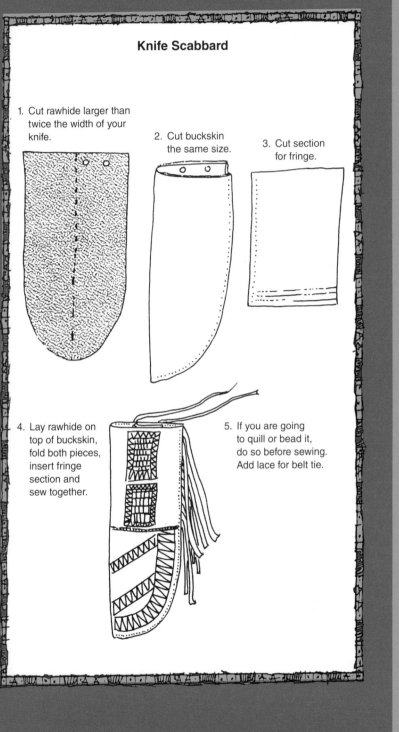

1. Cut rawhide larger than twice the width of your knife.

2. Cut buckskin the same size.

3. Cut section for fringe.

4. Lay rawhide on top of buckskin, fold both pieces, insert fringe section and sew together.

5. If you are going to quill or bead it, do so before sewing. Add lace for belt tie.

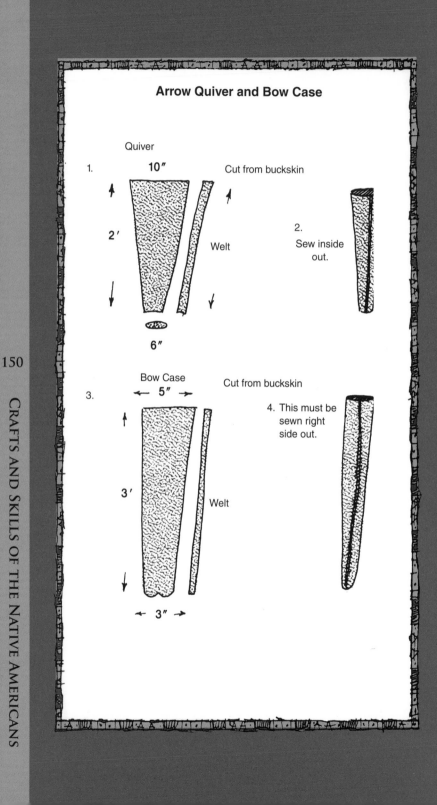

Arrow Quiver and Bow Case

Quiver

1. **10"** Cut from buckskin

2' Welt

6"

2. Sew inside out.

Bow Case Cut from buckskin

3. ← 5" →

3' Welt

← 3" →

4. This must be sewn right side out.

Arrow Quiver and Bow Case
(continued)

5. Shoulder strap and stick.
6. Cut ends for fringe.

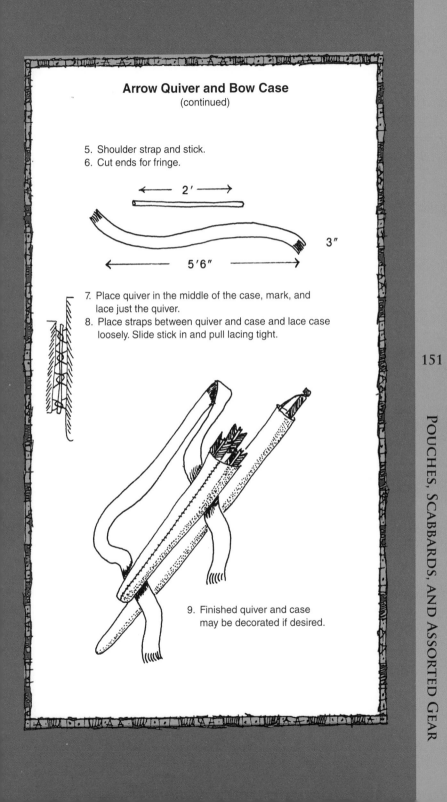

7. Place quiver in the middle of the case, mark, and lace just the quiver.
8. Place straps between quiver and case and lace case loosely. Slide stick in and pull lacing tight.

9. Finished quiver and case may be decorated if desired.

Awl Case

1. Cut pieces from scrap buckskin.

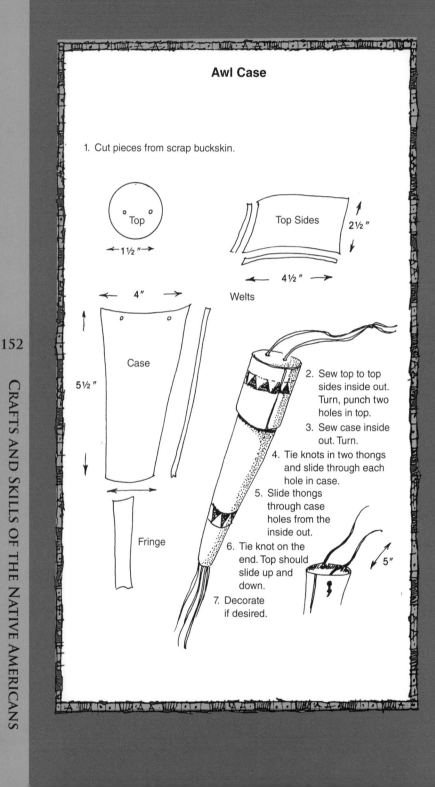

Top

← 1½" →

Top Sides

2½"

← 4½" →

Welts

← 4" →

Case

5½"

Fringe

2. Sew top to top sides inside out. Turn, punch two holes in top.

3. Sew case inside out. Turn.

4. Tie knots in two thongs and slide through each hole in case.

5. Slide thongs through case holes from the inside out.

6. Tie knot on the end. Top should slide up and down.

7. Decorate if desired.

5"

Parfleche Case

1. Use calf skin if possible. Cowhide is so thick it must be pounded very hard to get it to bend.
2. Cut rawhide to size you want.
3. Wet and fold. Set a board and heavy rocks on top to dry it under pressure.
4. Punch holes as shown.

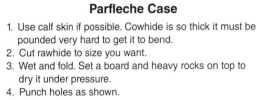

5. Lace through holes.
6. Paint geometric shapes.

Medicine Parfleche

1. Cut dry rawhide to desired size.
2. The front, back, and flap are all one piece.
3. insert uncut fringe piece between front and side.
4. Starting at front top edge, sew straight stitch around to the back. Repeat on other side.

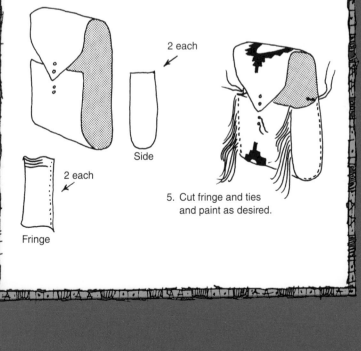

2 each

Side

2 each

Fringe

5. Cut fringe and ties and paint as desired.

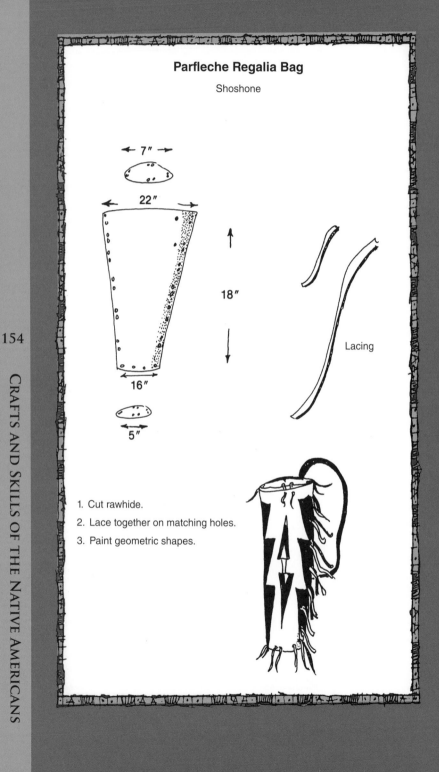

Parfleche Regalia Bag

Shoshone

7"

22"

18"

16"

5"

Lacing

1. Cut rawhide.
2. Lace together on matching holes.
3. Paint geometric shapes.

Parfleche Box

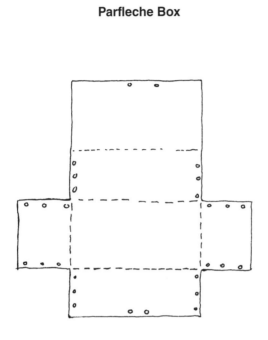

1. Rawhide boxes can be made in any size. Make a pattern on paper then cut to size.

2. Dampen rawhide to fold as shown on dotted lines.

3. Lace together at matching holes.

4. Decorate box with dye, acrylic paint, or leave it plain.

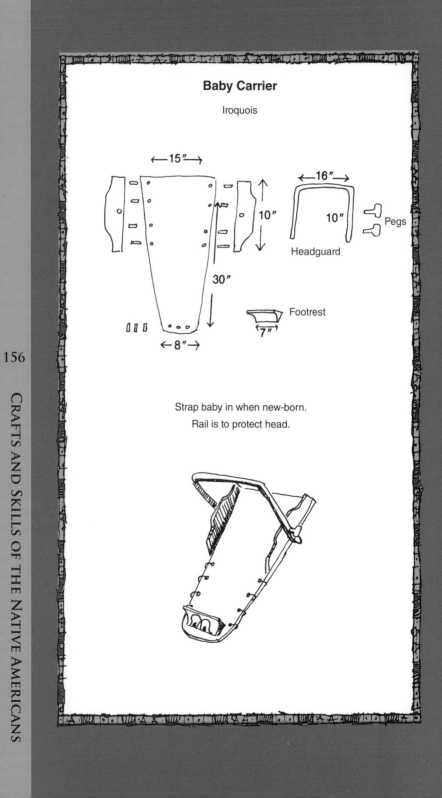

Baby Carrier

Iroquois

← 15″ →

10″

30″

← 8″ →

← 16″ →

10″

Pegs

Headguard

Footrest

7″

Strap baby in when new-born.
Rail is to protect head.

Ceremonial Pipe

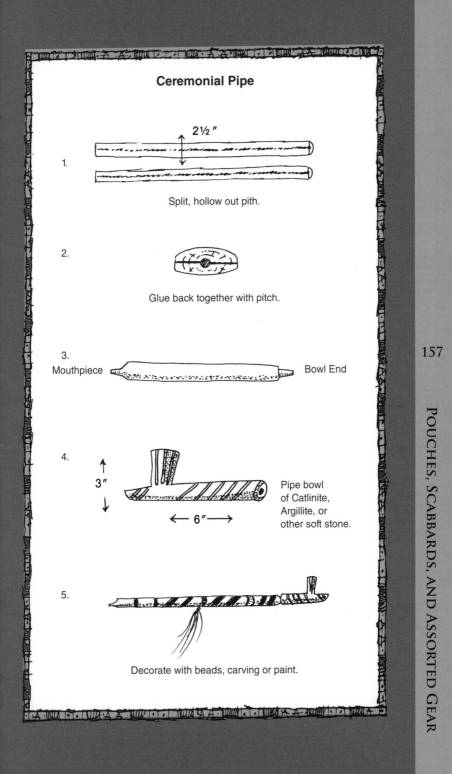

1. **2½"**

   Split, hollow out pith.

2. Glue back together with pitch.

3. Mouthpiece — Bowl End

4. **3"** ← **6"** →

   Pipe bowl
   of Catlinite,
   Argillite, or
   other soft stone.

5. Decorate with beads, carving or paint.

157

Willow Backrest

Native Americans used willow chairs in their tipis as a backrest. They are very convenient for modern use because they are easily portable. Our modern folding chairs are also nice, but they don't exactly fit the tipi atmosphere. When choosing willows for your chair, it is important to find the type of willow illustrated on the left. They grow in large, dense stands but not in single clumps. Cut the willow at the base and strip the bark off the same day for a smoother surface. You may want to leave the bark on for design purposes. However, the stripped willows make a prettier chair. Assemble the chair after the sticks have had sufficient time to dry. It is also necessary to trim off the knobs left from the branch joints after they have dried.

The tripod poles are made from the tips of lodgepole pine; other similar woods do as well, as long as they have the strength to hold when you put your backrest on it and lean back.

The Native American would also take two 6" poles that are 3"–4" around, lay them down and stake them wide enough apart to lay the back rest on full length and use it as their bed by laying furs on it for cushion and it would keep them off the damp ground. This also got rid of any little rock spots that can cause misery when trying to sleep.

You may want to make them smaller. If so, just reduce the size to fit your convenience. Once you've got the sticks peeled, dried, and trimmed, the rest is easy and quick, taking only about a day to complete.

Willow Backrest

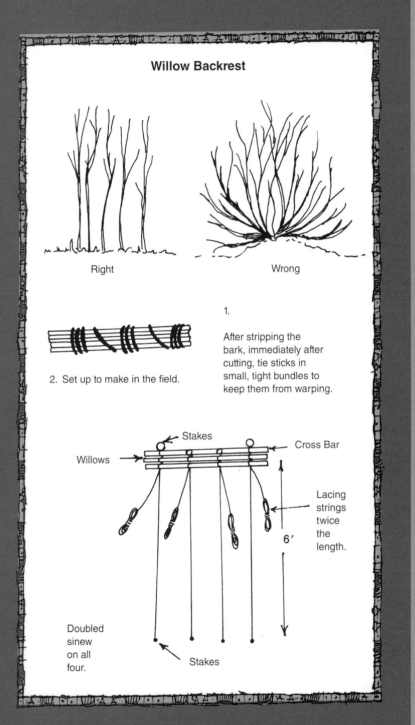

Right

Wrong

1.

After stripping the bark, immediately after cutting, tie sticks in small, tight bundles to keep them from warping.

2. Set up to make in the field.

Stakes

Willows

Cross Bar

Lacing strings twice the length.

6′

Doubled sinew on all four.

Stakes

Willow Backrest
(continued)

3. Place each willow with a thick end next to a small end.

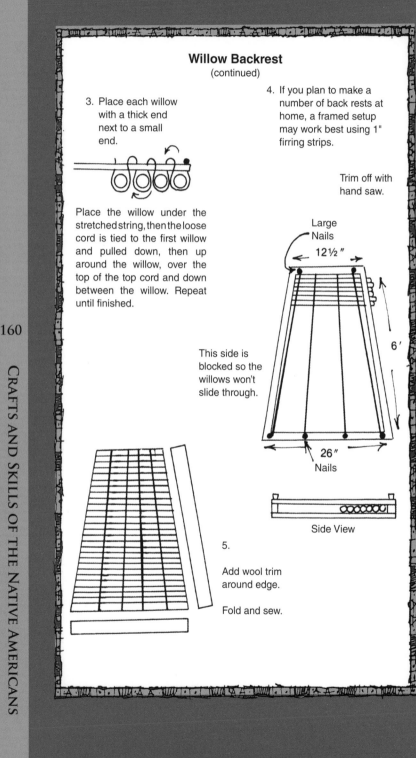

Place the willow under the stretched string, then the loose cord is tied to the first willow and pulled down, then up around the willow, over the top of the top cord and down between the willow. Repeat until finished.

4. If you plan to make a number of back rests at home, a framed setup may work best using 1" firring strips.

Trim off with hand saw.

Large Nails

12½"

6'

This side is blocked so the willows won't slide through.

26"

Nails

Side View

5.

Add wool trim around edge.

Fold and sew.

CRAFTS AND SKILLS OF THE NATIVE AMERICANS

Willow Backrest
(continued)

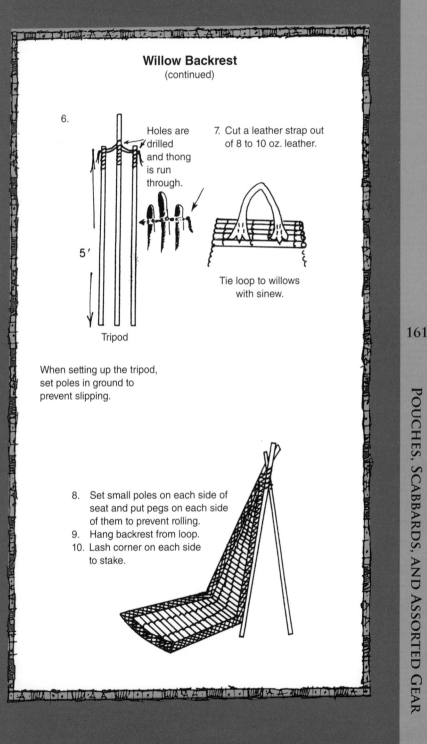

6.

Holes are drilled and thong is run through.

5'

Tripod

When setting up the tripod, set poles in ground to prevent slipping.

7. Cut a leather strap out of 8 to 10 oz. leather.

Tie loop to willows with sinew.

8. Set small poles on each side of seat and put pegs on each side of them to prevent rolling.
9. Hang backrest from loop.
10. Lash corner on each side to stake.

161

P ersonal adornment has been a part of every culture since the beginning of time: bone, stone, metal, and glass were turned into jewelry. The Native American has created unique and beautiful works of art from those substances. Both men and women wore necklaces, bracelets, hair pieces, and earrings. Shell was collected and used by the coastal tribes, then traded with inland Native Americans so that seashells were used across the continent. Some of the ornaments and jewelry shown in this chapter have no instructions on how to make them, because that alone would require a whole book on silversmithing. Others are simple enough to put together just by looking at the example.

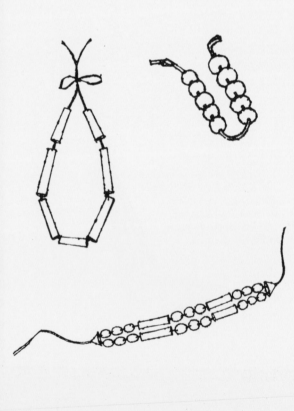

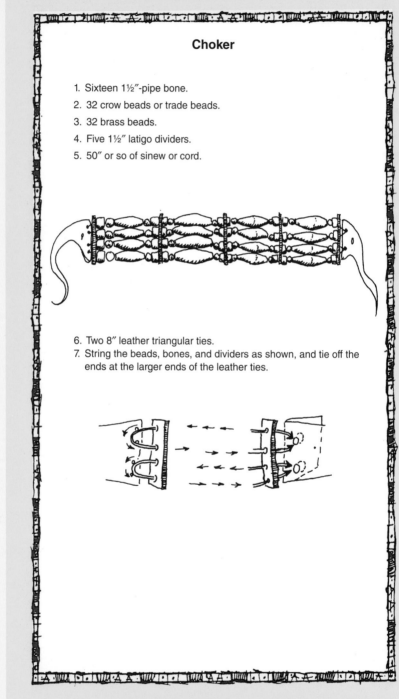

Choker

1. Sixteen 1½"-pipe bone.
2. 32 crow beads or trade beads.
3. 32 brass beads.
4. Five 1½" latigo dividers.
5. 50" or so of sinew or cord.

6. Two 8" leather triangular ties.
7. String the beads, bones, and dividers as shown, and tie off the ends at the larger ends of the leather ties.

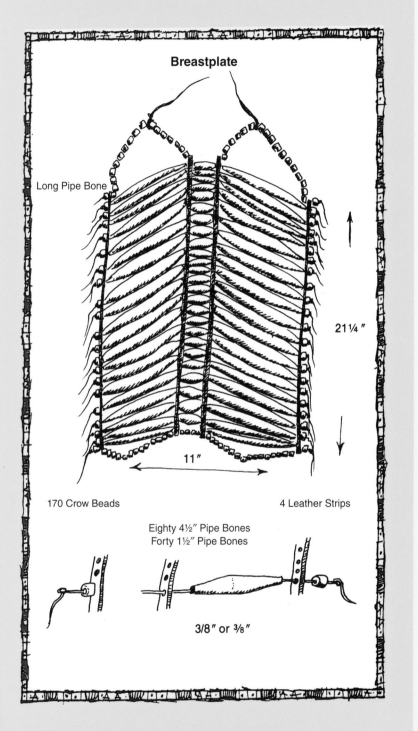

Breastplate

Long Pipe Bone

21¼″

11″

170 Crow Beads

4 Leather Strips

Eighty 4½″ Pipe Bones
Forty 1½″ Pipe Bones

3/8″ or ⅜″

Bead Designs

Morning Star	Star	Elk Hoof	Tipi
Spider	Cray Fish	Head	Buffalo Skull
Horse Tracks	Arrow Points	Dragonfly	Trails
Tipi	Rock	Leaf	Feather
Clouds	River with Island	Lightning	Sun

CRAFTS AND SKILLS OF THE NATIVE AMERICANS

Bead Designs
(continued)

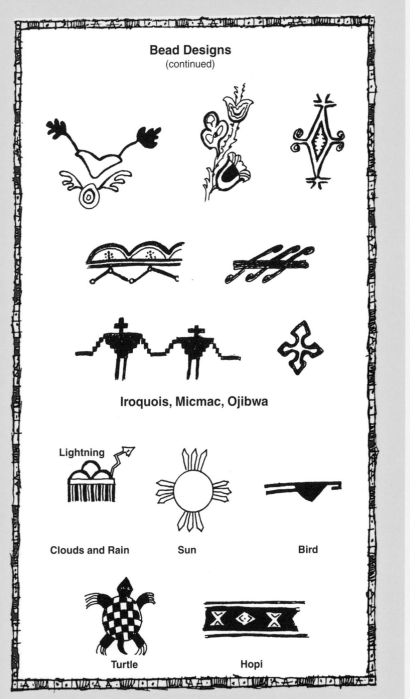

Iroquois, Micmac, Ojibwa

Lightning

Clouds and Rain

Sun

Bird

Turtle

Hopi

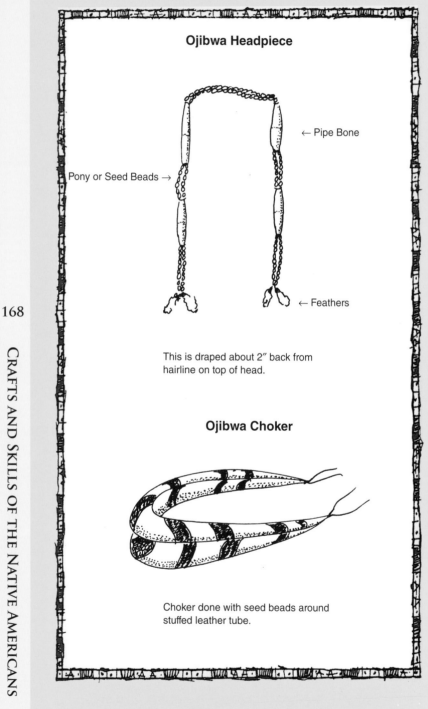

Ojibwa Headpiece

← Pipe Bone

Pony or Seed Beads →

← Feathers

This is draped about 2″ back from
hairline on top of head.

Ojibwa Choker

Choker done with seed beads around
stuffed leather tube.

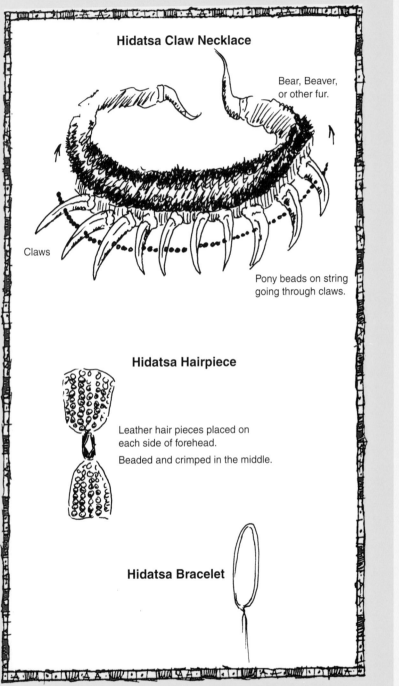

Hidatsa Claw Necklace

Bear, Beaver, or other fur.

Claws

Pony beads on string going through claws.

Hidatsa Hairpiece

Leather hair pieces placed on each side of forehead.

Beaded and crimped in the middle.

Hidatsa Bracelet

JEWELRY AND ORNAMENTS

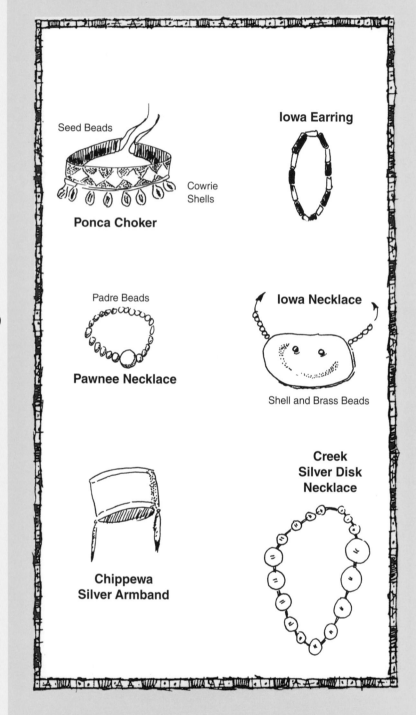

Seed Beads

Cowrie Shells

Ponca Choker

Iowa Earring

Padre Beads

Pawnee Necklace

Iowa Necklace

Shell and Brass Beads

Creek Silver Disk Necklace

Chippewa Silver Armband

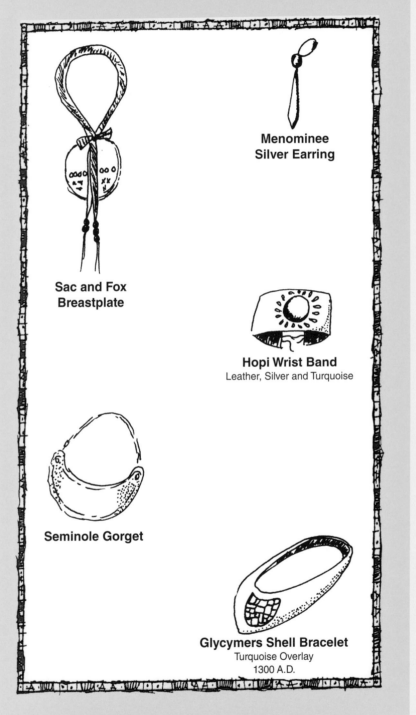

**Menominee
Silver Earring**

**Sac and Fox
Breastplate**

Hopi Wrist Band
Leather, Silver and Turquoise

Seminole Gorget

Glycymers Shell Bracelet
Turquoise Overlay
1300 A.D.

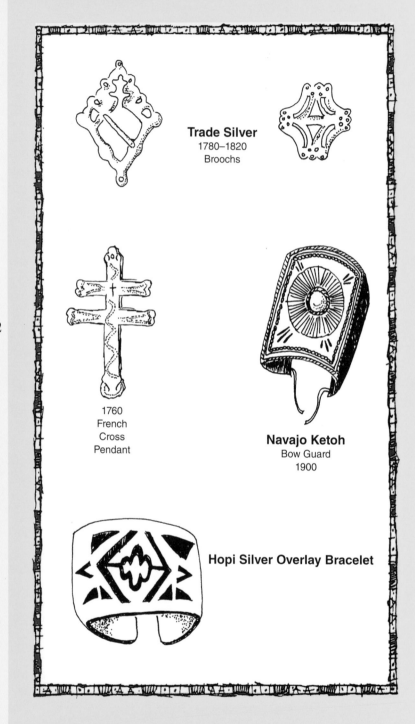

Trade Silver
1780–1820
Broochs

1760
French
Cross
Pendant

Navajo Ketoh
Bow Guard
1900

Hopi Silver Overlay Bracelet

Navajo Concho Belt

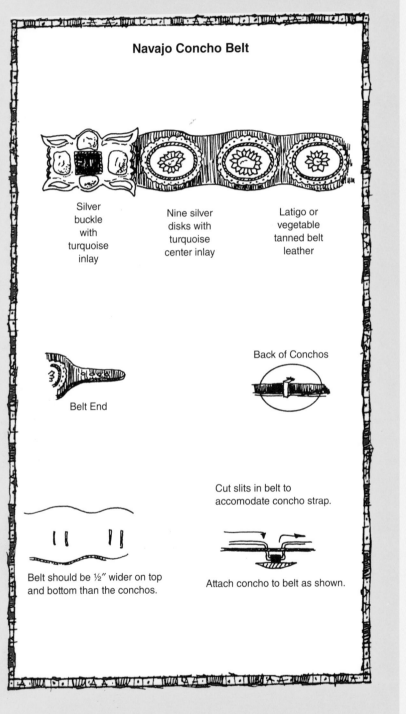

Silver buckle with turquoise inlay

Nine silver disks with turquoise center inlay

Latigo or vegetable tanned belt leather

Belt End

Back of Conchos

Cut slits in belt to accomodate concho strap.

Belt should be ½" wider on top and bottom than the conchos.

Attach concho to belt as shown.

Beadwork dates back to Egyptian times. Glass beads were introduced to the New World in 1492. Spanish trade-beads were introduced in the southwest during explorations there and trappers from Hudson Bay Company introduced beads from the north.

About the oldest piece of beadwork known is a sash woven on a twined warp on a powder horn, which was presented to General Montgomery in 1761. It contains 7,000 black and white pony beads.

Many texts say seed beads were not introduced to the plains tribes until 1840, but various sources from Hudson Bay lists, excavation sites, and the records of Lewis and Clark show that the seed bead was in use by 1805. Most tribes had trade routes from the North to South and the East to West before the white man came to the Central Plains and it was not uncommon to find articles of northwest origin in the southwest regions.

Beadwork is now known and used by almost all tribes in the United States and it is very ornate. Most tribes can be identified by the designs and patterns in their beadwork.

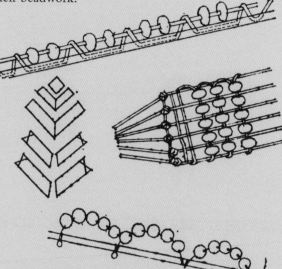

CHAPTER 12
BEAD AND QUILL WORK

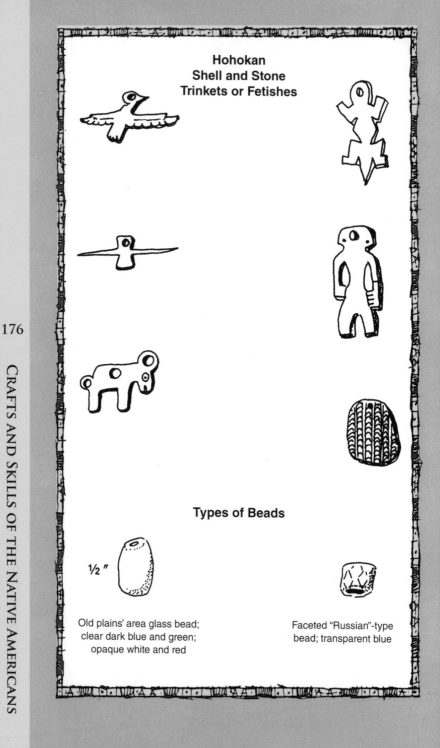

Hohokan Shell and Stone Trinkets or Fetishes

Types of Beads

½ "

Old plains' area glass bead; clear dark blue and green; opaque white and red

Faceted "Russian"-type bead; transparent blue

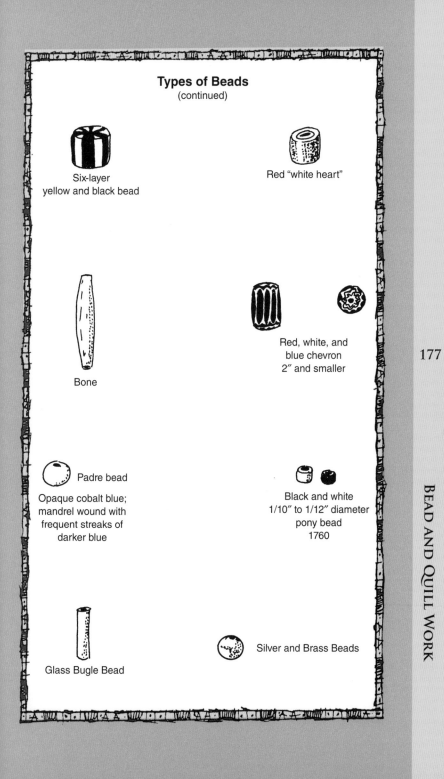

Types of Beads
(continued)

Six-layer
yellow and black bead

Red "white heart"

Bone

Red, white, and
blue chevron
2″ and smaller

Padre bead

Opaque cobalt blue;
mandrel wound with
frequent streaks of
darker blue

Black and white
1/10″ to 1/12″ diameter
pony bead
1760

Glass Bugle Bead

Silver and Brass Beads

177

BEAD AND QUILL WORK

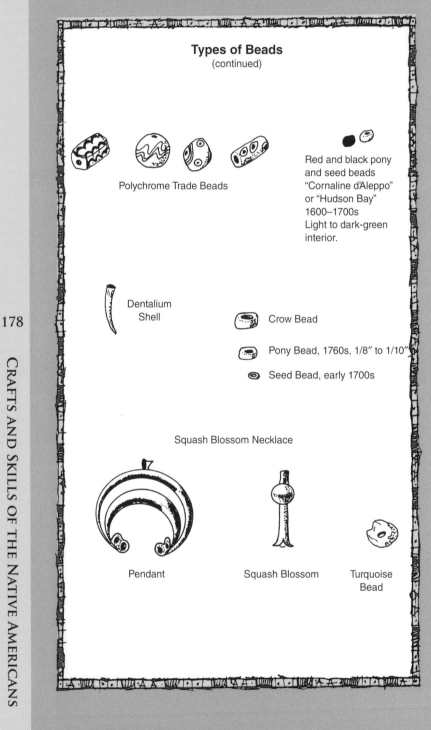

Types of Beads
(continued)

Polychrome Trade Beads

Red and black pony and seed beads "Cornaline d'Aleppo" or "Hudson Bay" 1600–1700s Light to dark-green interior.

Dentalium Shell

Crow Bead

Pony Bead, 1760s, 1/8″ to 1/10″

Seed Bead, early 1700s

Squash Blossom Necklace

Pendant

Squash Blossom

Turquoise Bead

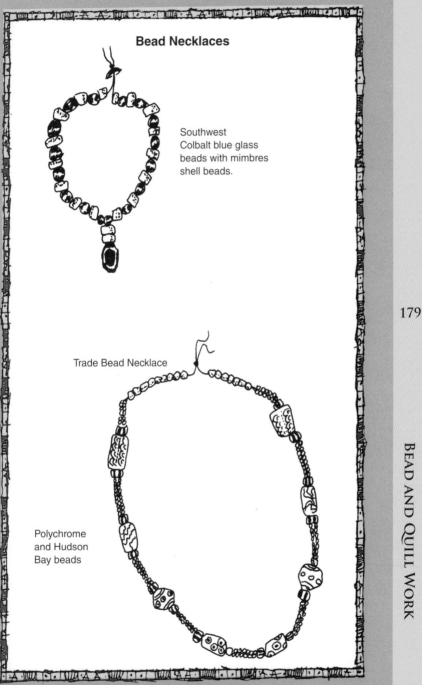

Bead Necklaces

Southwest
Colbalt blue glass
beads with mimbres
shell beads.

Trade Bead Necklace

Polychrome
and Hudson
Bay beads

BEAD AND QUILL WORK

Edge Beading

This type of beading is good for trim on cuffs of shirts, edges of hats, and on moccasins. It must be done with double thread.

1. Go down into the center of the bead with the thread into the leather and back out.
2. Slide an upright bead onto the thread, then a second one and repeat step one.

1. This is similar to lazy stitch.
2. Thread 4 to 6 beads then stitch into edge of leather and repeat.

1. For a diagonal beading pattern, start off the edge and string the beads.
2. Pull beads over the edge and sew back to the original side and repeat.

Beadwork for Strips and Moccasins

One of the most common types of beading is lazy stitch.

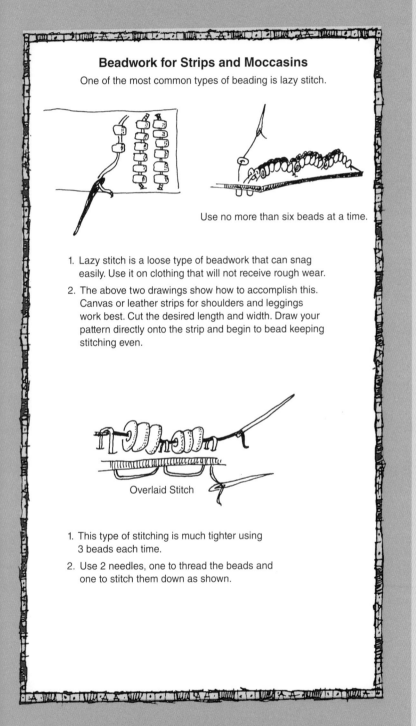

Use no more than six beads at a time.

1. Lazy stitch is a loose type of beadwork that can snag easily. Use it on clothing that will not receive rough wear.

2. The above two drawings show how to accomplish this. Canvas or leather strips for shoulders and leggings work best. Cut the desired length and width. Draw your pattern directly onto the strip and begin to bead keeping stitching even.

Overlaid Stitch

1. This type of stitching is much tighter using 3 beads each time.

2. Use 2 needles, one to thread the beads and one to stitch them down as shown.

Chippewa Cross-Warp Bead Weaving

1. Warp strands are stretched on the bow.

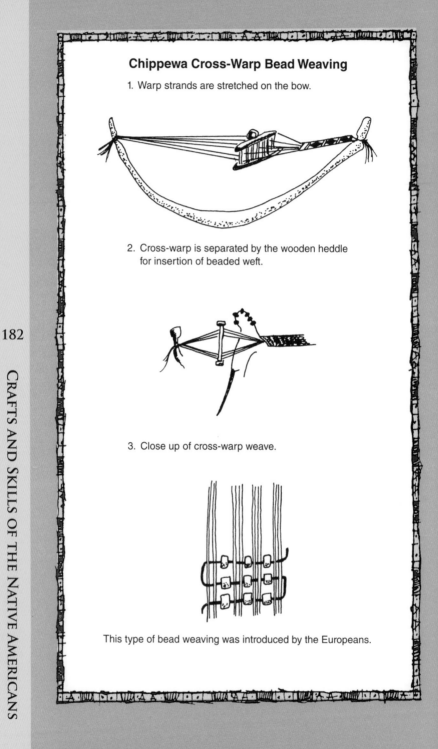

2. Cross-warp is separated by the wooden heddle for insertion of beaded weft.

3. Close up of cross-warp weave.

This type of bead weaving was introduced by the Europeans.

Double-Weft Bead Weaving

1. Warp strands are stretched on a common bead loom.
2. Pass one weft strand through beads above the warps.

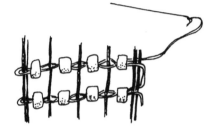

3. Come back through on the bottom.
4. Always set up an even number of warps so that the point or center of a design may be one bead.

Lakes Area

Spot-stitched patterns were done in concentric rows of shaded colors.

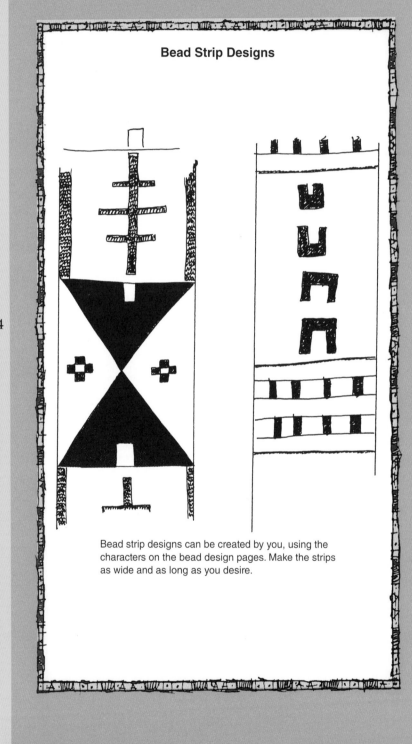

Bead Strip Designs

Bead strip designs can be created by you, using the
characters on the bead design pages. Make the strips
as wide and as long as you desire.

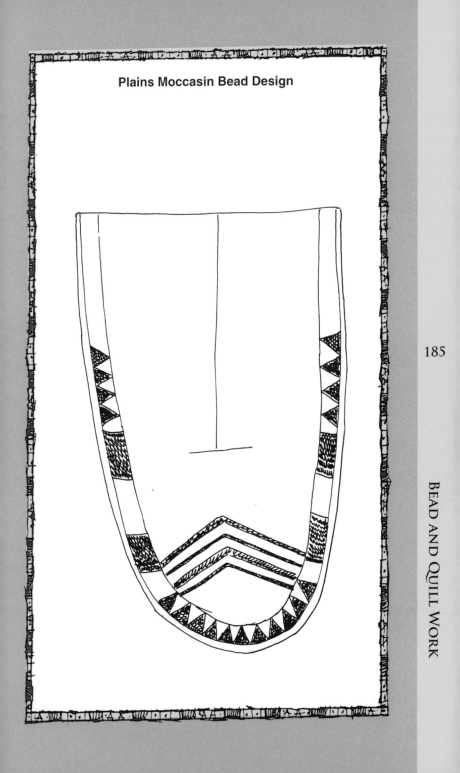

Plains Moccasin Bead Design

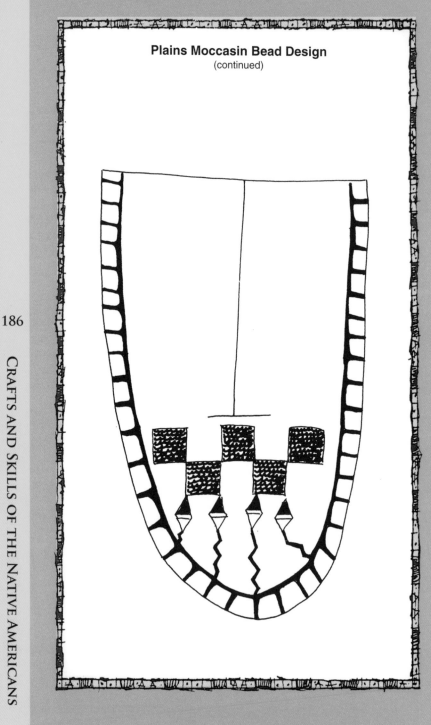

Plains Moccasin Bead Design
(continued)

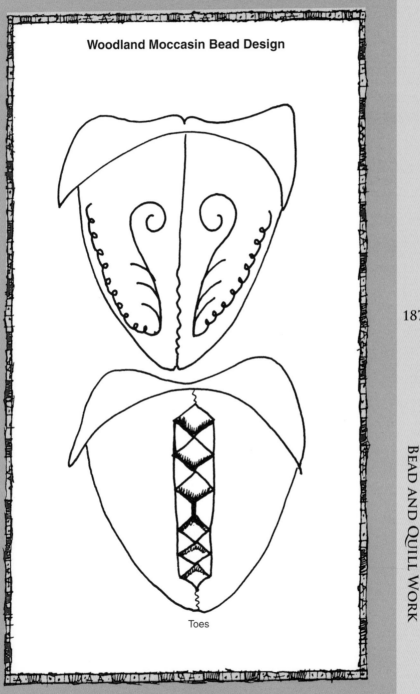

Woodland Moccasin Bead Design

Toes

Woodland Moccasin Bead Design
(continued)

Side View

Porcupine Quill Work

This work of fine decoration was distinctively done by the Native American. Style and application were different according to the locations of the tribes. The eastern tribes spread their works to the plains and then the plains tribes developed their own technique and created very beautiful geometric designs. The northeast tribes used single-thread wrap that resulted in fine colorful lines. The Cree wove their quills in such a way as to look like bead work.

Good Native American-craft stores will carry quills for sale or you may have to go to a Rendezvous or Pow Wow to buy them. If you are near an area where porcupine live, you can throw a large burlap bag on top of a live one, retrieve the bag and pick the quills out of it. Some states allow you to hunt porcupine and the meat and claws are useable as well as the tail of which a hair brush can be made.

Quill Plaiting

1. Use two parallel threads tied to article to be wrapped.
2. Tie other end to a small stick.
3. Use about a 2″ spacer-stick to keep threads taut.

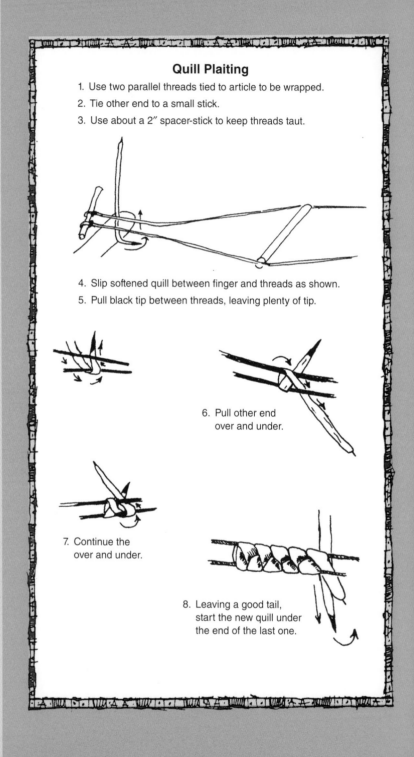

4. Slip softened quill between finger and threads as shown.
5. Pull black tip between threads, leaving plenty of tip.

6. Pull other end over and under.

7. Continue the over and under.

8. Leaving a good tail, start the new quill under the end of the last one.

Quill Plaiting
(continued)

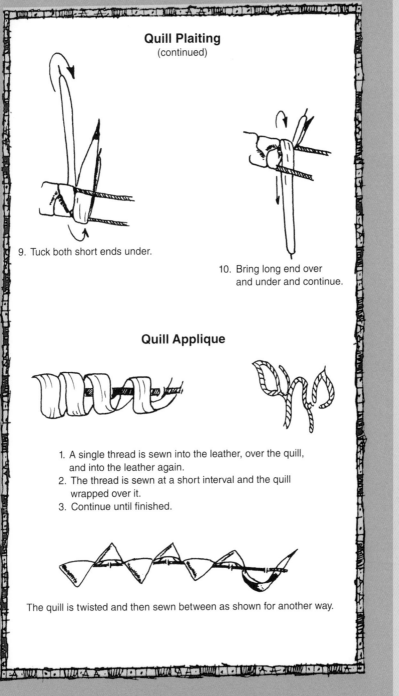

9. Tuck both short ends under.

10. Bring long end over and under and continue.

Quill Applique

1. A single thread is sewn into the leather, over the quill, and into the leather again.
2. The thread is sewn at a short interval and the quill wrapped over it.
3. Continue until finished.

The quill is twisted and then sewn between as shown for another way.

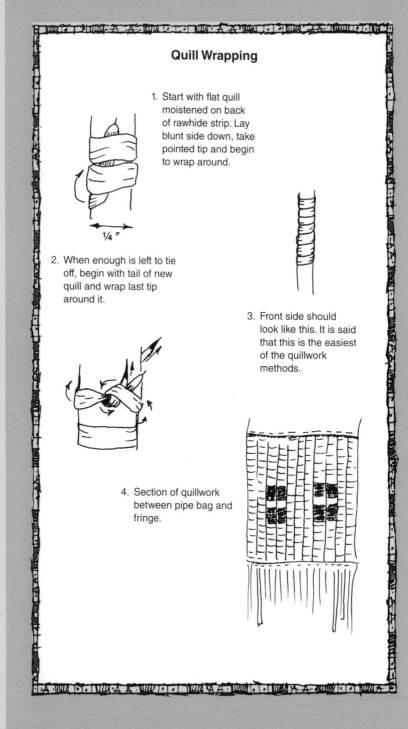

Quill Wrapping

1. Start with flat quill moistened on back of rawhide strip. Lay blunt side down, take pointed tip and begin to wrap around.

2. When enough is left to tie off, begin with tail of new quill and wrap last tip around it.

3. Front side should look like this. It is said that this is the easiest of the quillwork methods.

4. Section of quillwork between pipe bag and fringe.

¼ "

Two-String Quill Wrap

1. Draw pattern on leather.
2. Rows can be from ¼″ to ½″ wide.

3. Start top and bottom thread along the drawn lines.
4. Lay quill down, sew over top and fold quill down.
5. Sew over top again and fold up.

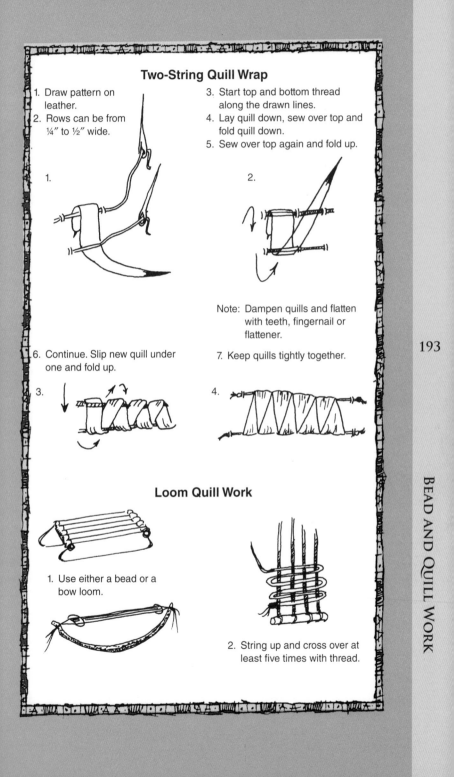

1.

2.

Note: Dampen quills and flatten with teeth, fingernail or flattener.

6. Continue. Slip new quill under one and fold up.

7. Keep quills tightly together.

3.

4.

Loom Quill Work

1. Use either a bead or a bow loom.

2. String up and cross over at least five times with thread.

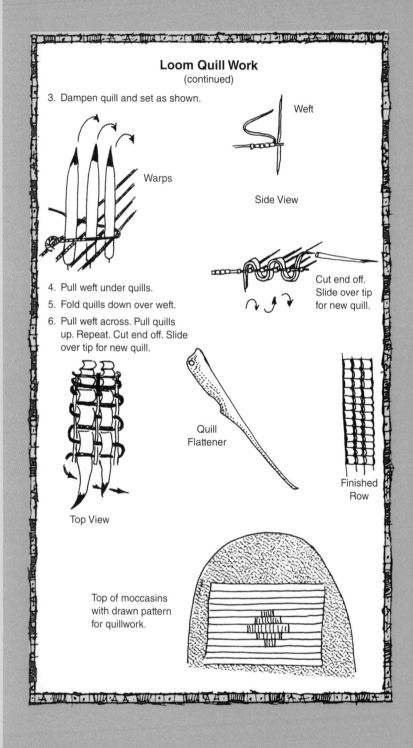

Loom Quill Work
(continued)

3. Dampen quill and set as shown.

Weft

Warps

Side View

4. Pull weft under quills.
5. Fold quills down over weft.
6. Pull weft across. Pull quills up. Repeat. Cut end off. Slide over tip for new quill.

Cut end off. Slide over tip for new quill.

Quill Flattener

Finished Row

Top View

Top of moccasins with drawn pattern for quillwork.

Quill Dying

Native Americans used dyes to color their quills derived from plants such as bloodroot, wild plum bark, blueberries, butternut, green hazelnut, alder, goldthread root, walnut juice, the root and bark of mountain mahogany and clay for yellow ochre to name a few. Today most quills are dyed with commercial dyes such as Rit.

To dye, clean the quills with a good cleanser. Make a mixture of a spoonful of sugar in about one-fourth gallon of hot water and about one-eighth bottle of liquid dye. Add the quills and heat over a low flame until the quills are colored to the shade desired. Rinse them off with cold water and store them in a container with a lid. You may want to separate the quills according to size to make your quilling easier. Always remember that quills can cause great pain if you step on them or sit on them so be careful not to leave any lying around.

N o life is complete without games and music even in the harshest society and its surroundings. The Native Americans made games of bone, wood, and leather. Stories were told to carry on traditions not only because of the lack of a written language but for their sheer enjoyment of good tales. These tales were often sung.

Games were not just for children, but for adults as well. Betting was a serious enough sport that it was not uncommon to lose a wife or a horse in wagers on the games. (I would suggest you don't go that far!) Tops and buzzers, which many suppose to be fairly modern toys, were used by the American Indians many years ago.

Musical instruments were used for dances, singing, and ceremonies. Various types of drums, rattles, maracas, and whistles were used together to create a rhythm somewhat different from our music of today. Rattles, drum, and whistle are illustrated here for your use.

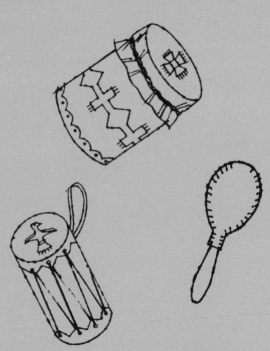

CHAPTER 13

MUSICAL INSTRUMENTS AND GAMES

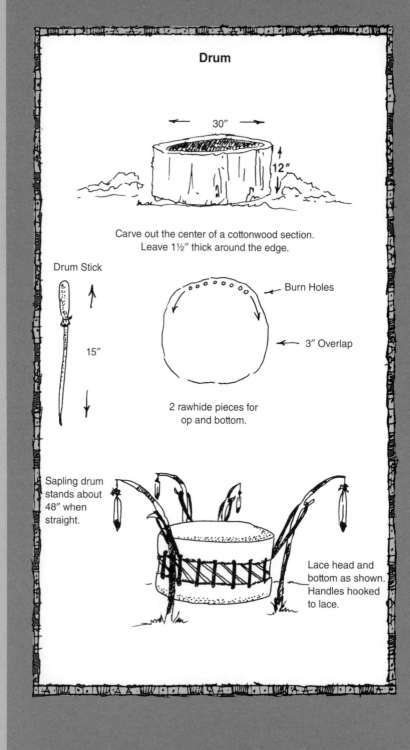

Drum

30″

12″

Carve out the center of a cottonwood section.
Leave 1½″ thick around the edge.

Drum Stick

15″

Burn Holes

3″ Overlap

2 rawhide pieces for
op and bottom.

Sapling drum
stands about
48″ when
straight.

Lace head and
bottom as shown.
Handles hooked
to lace.

CRAFTS AND SKILLS OF THE NATIVE AMERICANS

Gourd Rattle

Different types of gourds

Drill hole in the gourd.
Empty shell of seeds with wire.
Drill hole on top.
Fill with sand.

Pegs

Handle

Assemble; put pegs
in top and bottom.

Turtle Shell Rattle

Rawhide
lace open
end

Clean out shell. Fill with
alum and salt to cure.

Lace Handle

Fill with
sand.

Cut wooden handle
to go on neck.

Bone Whistle

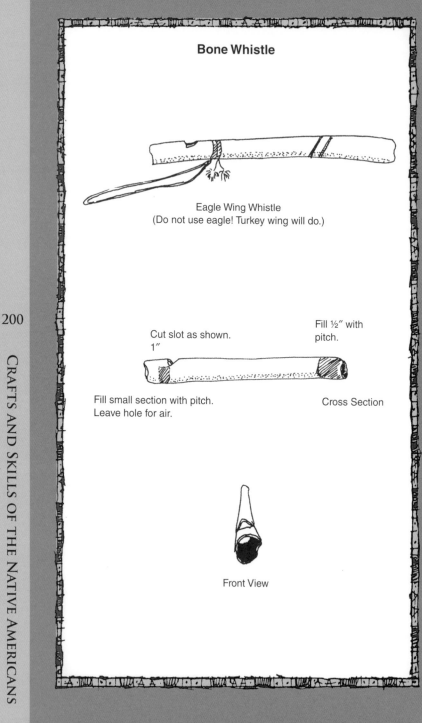

Eagle Wing Whistle
(Do not use eagle! Turkey wing will do.)

Cut slot as shown.
1″

Fill ½″ with
pitch.

Fill small section with pitch.
Leave hole for air.

Cross Section

Front View

Ring and Pin Game

Cree, Kawchodinne, Sauk, and Hupa

This game is played by holding pin in hand and flipping the leather tab and horn ends or dew claws up seeing if you can snare an end as well as a hole in the tab. The center hole is the highest point.

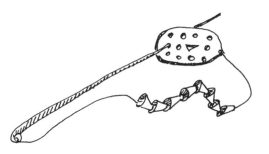

Buzz

This is a whirling device made of shell, wood, or antler. Two holes fairly close together are drilled then twine or sinew is passed through them, and the end tied off making a loop on each end to pass the fingers through. The disk is flipped around till the string is twisted, then pulled in and out. The disk will whirl.

Snow Snake

This is a winter game. Each player has one throwing stick.

1. Grasp throwing stick's small end with thumb and three fingers, placing the fourth finger on the end.
2. Throw below waist.
3. Pack snow to make a long trough or throw it on the ice.
4. The winner throws his stick the farthest.

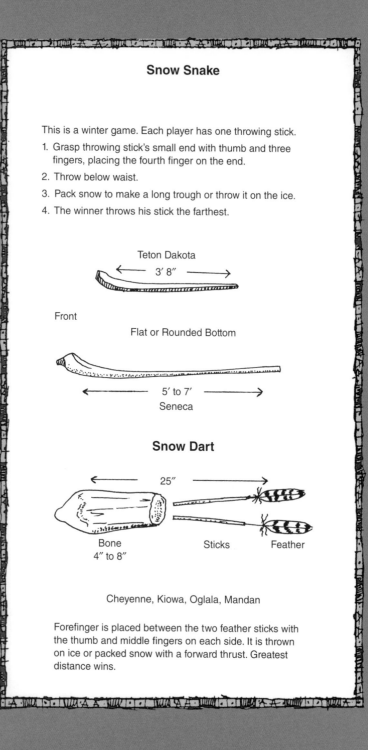

Teton Dakota

←—— 3′ 8″ ——→

Front

Flat or Rounded Bottom

←——— 5′ to 7′ ———→
Seneca

Snow Dart

←——— 25″ ———→

Bone
4″ to 8″

Sticks

Feather

Cheyenne, Kiowa, Oglala, Mandan

Forefinger is placed between the two feather sticks with the thumb and middle fingers on each side. It is thrown on ice or packed snow with a forward thrust. Greatest distance wins.

Hoop and Pole

Chipewa, Gros Ventre, Apache, Pawnee, Cheyenne, and Arapaho

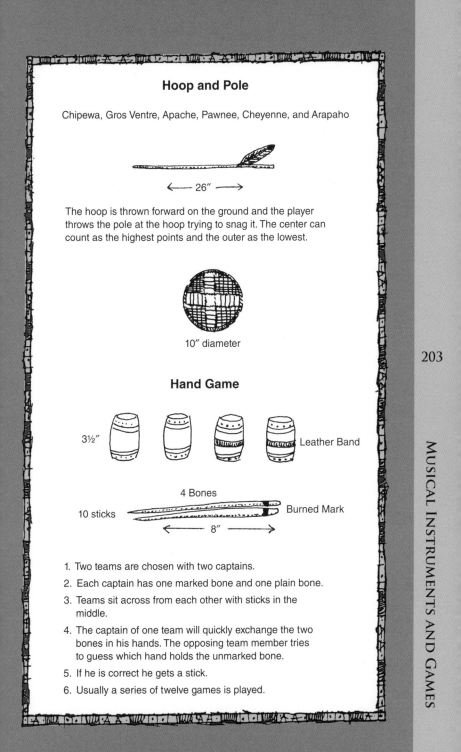

← 26″ →

The hoop is thrown forward on the ground and the player throws the pole at the hoop trying to snag it. The center can count as the highest points and the outer as the lowest.

10″ diameter

Hand Game

3½″   Leather Band

4 Bones

10 sticks   Burned Mark

← 8″ →

1. Two teams are chosen with two captains.
2. Each captain has one marked bone and one plain bone.
3. Teams sit across from each other with sticks in the middle.
4. The captain of one team will quickly exchange the two bones in his hands. The opposing team member tries to guess which hand holds the unmarked bone.
5. If he is correct he gets a stick.
6. Usually a series of twelve games is played.

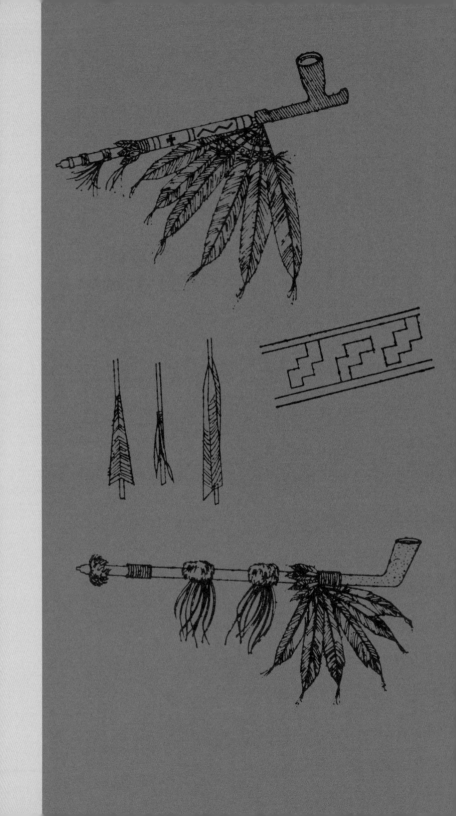

GLOSSARY

Anasazi	Southwest tribe, extinct.
Applique	Sewing beads tightly to material.
Arrow	Projectile shot with bow.
Arrow point	Stone or metal point inserted in shaft.
Arrow shaft	Portion that holds the fletching and point.
Atlatl	Bar for throwing spear.
Beaming Tool	Implement to flesh hides.
Billet	Elk antler used for knaping stone for points.
Birch bark	Bark of the birch tree used for dwellings, boats and boxes.
Blow gun	Hollow tube used to blow a dart at object.
Bone awl	Sharpened bone for leather hole punching.
Bonnet	Feathered Indian hat.
Bow	Sinew-backed slender wood strung to shoot arrows.
Bow drill fire	Fire created by friction sticks.
Braining	Process of applying brain to hide for tanning.
Breast plate	Bone or bead rows tied in rows hung from neck.
Breech clout	Strip of cloth or leather worn between legs.
Buckskin	Tanned hides of deer.
Bull boat	Cup-shaped boat of hide and saplings, hard to steer.
Calico	Small flower-patterned cotton material.
Canoe	Boat with tapered vertical flat ends.
Cantle	Back portion of saddle against your seat.
Capote	Wool coat made of wool.
Cedar posts	Poles of the cedar tree used in pit dwellings.
Chevron bead	Striped glass bead.
Choker	Necklace tight against neck.

Cinch	Strap tied around horse to keep saddle on.
Clavical	Shoulder blade of animal or man.
Clove hitch	Type of knot to tie tripod poles of tipi.
Concho	Metal disks usually of silver to make belts.
Dew cloth	Liner of tipi essential to draw air.
Door Flap	Covering for tipi door.
Duck canvas	Rough thick cotton cloth.
Ermine	Same as the weasel only with winter coat.
Fat scraper	Sharpened bone to remove fat from hide.
Fetish	Small carved figures.
Fire pit	Heating and cooking source of Indian dwellings.
Fireboard	Spindle is driven into it by bow to create spark.
Flaking	Chipping points.
Flap poles	Two poles to stretch out smoke flaps.
Fleshing	Removing fat and meat from hide.
Fletching	Split and cut feathers for arrows.
Fringe	Thin strips cut to hang on clothing and bags.
Girth	Strap to tie down travois around horses chest.
Gorget	Crescent-shaped metal neck piece.
Gourd	Round shaped vegetable from vine used for cups and rattles.
Graining tool	Notched tool to work hide.
Green River	Knife made by said company.
Gunwale	Inner and outer wood trim.
Hammer stone	Stone held with fingers or handle for hammering.
Hands	Guessing game with sticks and bones.
Hawk	Small axe for throwing and cutting small limbs.
Heddle	Separates the warps for the weft insertion.
Hem	Material folded over with raw edge in and sewn down.
Jerky	Strips of dried meat.
Ketoh	Navajo bow guard.

Lacing Pins	Wooden pegs to hold the tipi together.
Lamintation	Strips of wood lashed together, bowed and put on ends of canoe.
Lance	Spear used for war or hunting.
Latigo	Heavy oil-soaked leather.
Lazy stitch	Loosely sewn bead technique.
Leggings	Pants without middle requiring a breechclout.
Leister	Fishing spear.
Lodge poles	Tall slender pine used for the tipi.
Loom	Frame for doing weaving or beadwork.
Mano	Hand-held stone used in connection with the metate.
Metal awl	Four-sided sharpened rod for punching holes.
Metate	Grinding stone.
Moccasins	Leather soft-sole shoes.
Nodule	Stone of flint, agate, obsidian, or slate for flaking.
Ozan	Inner roof of tipi.
Paddle	Used for rowing canoe.
Padre bead	Round, blue beads brought in by Spaniards.
Parfleche	Containers of rawhide for carrying and storage.
Paunch	Stomach of animal.
Pecking stone	Large or small slender stone used to chip other stones.
Pemmican	Dried meat, ground and mixed with suet.
Pin holes	For insertion of lacing pins on tipi.
Pipe bag	Pouch to hold pipe and tobbacco.
Pit dwelling	Indian lodge dug into earth covered with thatch and sod.
Pitch	Pine gum.
Pommel	Front upright portion of saddle.
Pottery	Baked clay vessels.
Quill smoother	Implement to flatten porcupine quills.

Quillwork	Decorative work done with porcupine quills.
Quiver	Container to carry arrows.
Rain pegs	Small, wooden pegs used to keep space between liner and poles.
Rawhide	Hide of an animal, fleshed and cleaned with or without hair.
Regalia bag	Rawhide container for bonnets.
Ribs	Used to hold in sheathing on canoe.
Root digger	Slender pointed stick for obtaining plant roots.
Saddle	A seat or pad on a horse to sit upon.
Saddle bags	A bag put over cantle to carry belongings.
Sandstone	Soft pourous stone with sandpaper-like surface.
Saplings	Very young trees with bendable trunks.
Scraper	Elk or wood-handled blade to scrape hair off hides.
Sheath	Knife or rifle cover.
Sheathing	Strips of flat cedar tappered on ends.
Sinew	Tendons of animals used for sewing and wrapping.
Smoke flap	Section on tipi that can be shifted with the wind to draw smoke.
Smoking hide	Waterproofing hide.
Snow snake	Game stick thrown on ice or frozen snow.
Spindle	Drill portion of friction sticks.
Stem	Small flat triangular wood on top of ends of canoe to hold end.
Stirrup	Part of saddle to put feet in.
Strike-a-lite	Container to hold flint and steel.
Tanning	Preparation and process for making buckskin.
Tassel	Strip of long material hanging from clothes or saddles.
Thatch	Woven saplings.

Tinder	Bark of cottonwood, cedar, or sage to catch spark in firebuilding.
Tipi	Portable dwelling of Plains Indian.
Trade beads	Beads used by both whites and Indians for barter.
Trade blanket	Blankets obtained from white traders.
Trade silver	Very thin metal brooches stamped and rouletted of German silver.
Traps	Ways to catch animal, fowl, and fish.
Travois	A shaped frame pulled by horse or dog to carry belongings.
Warp	Vertical threads on the loom.
Weft	Horizontal threads on a loom.
Welt	Strip of leather sewn between two other pieces for reinforcement.
Whip stitch	Sewing stitch wrapped around edge.
Wigwam	Indian lodge made of sapling covered with bark.
Willow back rest	A mat made of willows with a tripod to hold up back.
Wither	Top of shoulder of a horse.

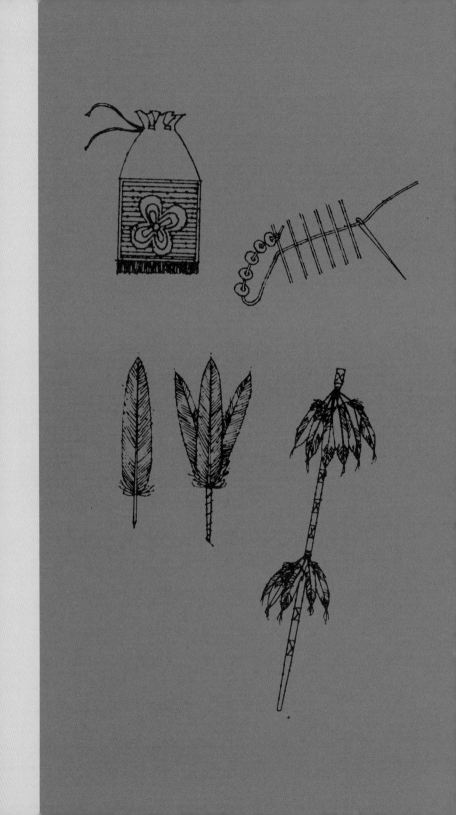

ANNOTATED BIBLIOGRAPHY OF SELECTED BOOKS

Abrams, Harry N. *The West of Buffalo Bill* (New York: Harry N. Abrams, Inc. Publishers), 289 pp. Contains three sections of Buffalo Bill Museum, Plains Indian Museum, and the Whitney Gallery of Western Art.

Adney, Edwin & Chapelle, Howard. *The Bark Canoes and Skin Boats of North America* (Washington, U.S. Government Printing Office, 1964), *Smithsonian Institute*, 242 pp. A very concise book of drawings and instructions on the building of canoes and kayaks.

Ahlbron, Richard E. *Man-Made Mobile—Early Saddles of Western North America* (Washington: Smithsonian Institution Press, 1980), 147 pp. Photographs and history of western saddlery of the Indian and the white men.

Appleton, Leroy H. *American Indian Design and Decoration* (New York: Dover Publications, 1971), 277 pp. 700 drawings with stories from various tribes.

Baldwin, Gordon C. *How Indians Really Lived* (New York: G. P. Putnam's Sons, 1967), 233 pp. Contains black and white photographs and a good general survey of the history of the American Indian.

Belitz, Larry. *Brain Tanning the Sioux Way* (Hot Springs: 1979), 16 pp. Written for knowledgeable tanners, lacks some important steps.

Capps, Benjamin. *The Indians* (Alexandria: Time-Life Books, Inc.), 240 pp. Well-illustrated in-depth view of the lives

and confrontations of the American Indians. Color
photography.

Culin, Stewart. *Games of the North American Indians* (New
York: Dover Publications Inc., 1975), 846 pp. The most
comprehensive book on Indian games that is in print; very
well researched, illustrated and written.

Densmore, Frances. *How Indians Use Wild Plants for Food, Medicine
& Crafts* (New York: Dover Publications, Inc., 1974), 114 pp.
A good technical book with charts of plant names and their
uses.

Dockstader, Fredrick J. *Indian Art in America* (Greenwich: 1961).
Illustrated works of Indian art and commentary.

Gilbert, E. W. *The Exploration of Western America 1800–1850* (New
York: Cooper Publishers, 1966), 233 pp. An account of the
Indians, Lewis and Clark and the fur trade of the Americans
and British.

Grant, Bruce. *American Indians, Yesterday and Today* (New York: E. P.
Dutton & Co., Inc., 1960), 352 pp. An encyclopedia of Indian
names, customs, etc., with short explanations.

Grinnell, George Bird. *Blackfoot Lodge Tales* (Lincoln/London:
University of Nebraska Press, 1962), 310 pp. Adventure,
ancient times, social life, hunting, and other stories which
give an overview of the life of the Blackfoot Indian.

Hassrick, Royal B. *The George Catlin Book of American Indians*
(New York: Promontory Press, 1981), 206 pp. Short
introduction with captioned color plates of Catlin's works as
he traveled the West in the 1830s.

Hudson, Charles. *The Southeastern Indians* (Knoxville: University
of Tennessee Press, 1978), 573 pp. Contains history, religion,
social organization and crafts. There are few illustrations but it
is well-written and researched.

Hunt, W. Ben. *Indian Silver Smithing* (London: Collier MacMillan Pub., 1960), 160 pp. An elaborately illustrated book on how to do silver smithing.

Kennard, A. Edward. *Hopi Kachinas* (New York: Museum of the American Indians Heye Foundation, 1971), 120 pp. The history and role of Kachinas in Hopi life with color illustrations.

Ketchum, William C. *Western Memorabilia Collectables of the Old West* (Maplewood: Rutledge Book, Hammond Inc., 1980), 256 pp. Types and styles of collectable western items with a price guide. A good resource manual for collectors.

LaFarge, Oliver. *A Pictorial History of the American Indian* (New York: Crown Publishers, Inc., 1974), 288 pp. A good cross section of history and pictures of Indians then and now.

Lyford, Carrie A. *Quill and Beadwork of the Western Sioux* (Boulder: Johnson Publishing Co., 1979), 116 pp. Illustrated techniques of quillwork and beadwork with patterns to use.

Lowie, R. H. *Indians of the Plains* (New York: McGraw-Hill, 1954). Written summary of life and travels of the Plains Indians.

Mails, Thomas E. *The Mystic Warriors of the Plains* (New York: Doubleday & Co., 1972), 618 pp. Well Illustrated and written book on religion, social customs, clothing, etc., of the Plains Indians.

Mails, Thomas E. *The People Called Apache* (Englewood Cliffs: Prentice-Hall, Inc., 1974), 447 pp. Exceptional drawings and well-researched book on the life and history of the Apache.

Mason, Bernard S. *The Book of Indian Crafts and Costumes* (New York: The Ronald Press Co., 1946), 116 pp. Illustrated Indian Crafts.

Mason, Otis. *Aboriginal Skin-Dressing* (Seattle: The Shorey Book Store, 1971), 100 pp. The best historically documented book on Indian and Eskimo tanning tools and methods based on material in the U.S. National Museum. Illustrated.

Miles, Charles. *Indian & Eskimo Artifacts of North America* (New York: Bonanza Books, 1973), 243 pp. Numerous photographed artifacts of tools, weapons, travel, games, and musical instruments.

Murphy, Dan. *Lewis and Clark Voyage of Discovery* (Las Vegas: K. C. Publications, 1977), 64 pp. Color photography by famous David Muench shows a pictorial trip of Lewis and Clark as Dan Murphy takes excerpts from the journals and recreates the expedition.

Naylor, Mario. *Authentic Indian Designs* (New York: Dover Publications, Inc., 1975), 219 pp. 2500 drawings and photos from reports of the Bureau of American Ethonology on pottery, baskets, pouches, etc.

Salomon, Julian H. *The Book of Indian Crafts and Indian Lore* (New York: Harper & Row Publishers, 1928), 418 pp. Illustrated lightly with extensive body copy which is well-written. A good selection of Indian names and meanings.

Scholz-Peters, Ruth. *Indian Bead Stringing and Weaving* (New York: Sterling Publishing, 1974), 63 pp. Basic illustrated book on beading.

Sides, Dorothy Smith. *Decorative Art of the Southwestern Indians* (New York: Dover Publications, 1961). 50 plates of illustrations of pottery and blanket designs.

Sorensen, Cloyd. "Glass Trade Beads" *Arizona Highways.* (Phoenix: July, 1971), 28 pp. Most pages in color; history and photographs of original trade beads.

Turner, Geoffrey. *Indians of North America* (Blandford Press Ltd., 1979), 261 pp. A good cross section of Indian history and living. Illustrated and sectioned by tribe.

Waldorf, D. C. *The Art of Flint Knapping* (Cassville: Litho Printers, 1979), 52 pp. Step-by-step illustrated instructions on various methods of making arrowheads and spear points.

White, George M. *Craft Manual of Northwest Indian Beading* (Ronan: 1972), 163 pp. Illustrated pages of techniques, patterns and designs of beadwork.

Whitford, Andrew H. *North American Indian Arts* (New York: Golden Press Publishing Inc., 1970), 160 pp. Small color drawings of crafts and explanations of each. Very good.

Wright, Barton. *Hopi Kachinas* (Flagstaff: Northland Press, 1977), 129 pp. Photographed guide to collecting Kachina dolls. It explains the names and functions of the dolls.

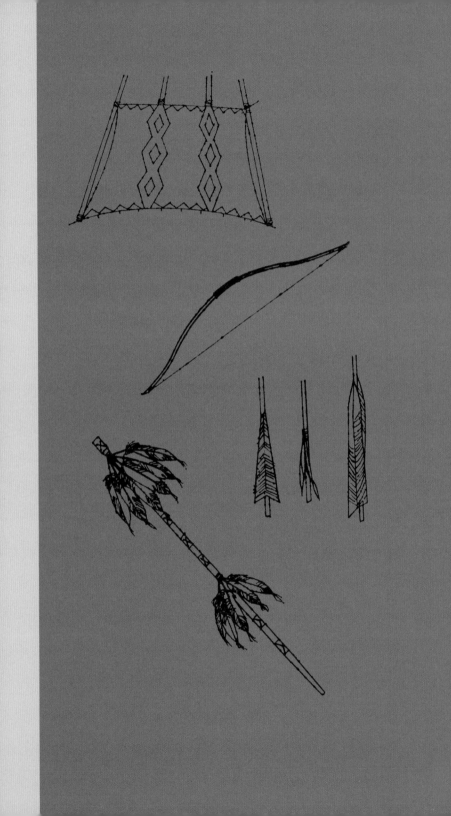